CRYSTAL
Lore, Legends & Myths

The Fascinating History of the
World's Most Powerful Gems
and Stones

Athena Perrakis, Ph.D.
Founder of Sage Goddess

FAIR WINDS

Brimming with creative inspiration, how-to projects, and useful information to enrich your everyday life, Quarto Knows is a favorite destination for those pursuing their interests and passions. Visit our site and dig deeper with our books into your area of interest: Quarto Creates, Quarto Cooks, Quarto Homes, Quarto Lives, Quarto Drives, Quarto Explores, Quarto Gifts, or Quarto Kids.

First Published in 2019 by Fair Winds Press, an imprint of The Quarto Group,
100 Cummings Center, Suite 265-D, Beverly, MA 01915, USA.
T (978) 282-9590 F (978) 283-2742 QuartoKnows.com

Fair Winds Press titles are also available at discount for retail, wholesale, promotional, and bulk purchase. For details, contact the Special Sales Manager by email at specialsales@quarto.com or by mail at The Quarto Group, Attn: Special Sales Manager, 100 Cummings Center, Suite 265-D, Beverly, MA 01915, USA.

23 22 21 20 19   1 2 3 4 5

ISBN: 978-1-59233-841-2

Digital edition published in 2019
eISBN: 978-1-63159-518-9

Library of Congress Cataloging-in-Publication Data

Perrakis, Athena, author.
Crystal legends, lore & myths : the fascinating history of the world's
  most powerful gems and stones / Athena Perrakis, Ph.D.
ISBN 9781592338412 (hardcover book)
Crystals--Miscellanea.
LCC BF1442.C78 P47 2019 | DDC 133/.2548--dc23
LCCN 2018051104

Photography: Shutterstock, except page 24 James St. John, pages 27, 32, 151, 186
Sage Goddess, pages 71, 128, 169 Rob Lavinsky, iRocks.com – CC-BY-SA-3.0,
and page 136 Glenn Scott Photography

Printed in China

MIX
Paper from
responsible sources
FSC® C008047
www.fsc.org

I dedicate this book to the crystals themselves. Oh, how I love you and take pleasure in looking after you. Thank you for choosing me to steward and keep you. To my husband, David, and my children, Nick and Zoe, who are my gems. To my parents, who always indulged my love of gems, and to all of my students whose endless curiosity inspires my own. To my line and the goddesses from whom I descend: May the Great Mystery enchant all of us forever. A'ho.

CONTENTS

"But wee, not satisfied therewith, peirce deeper and enter into her very bowels . . . and for to seeke out gemmes and some little stones, we sinke pits deep within the ground. Thus wee plucke the very heart-strings out of her, and all to weare on our finger one, to fulfill our pleasure and desire. How many hands are worne with digging and delving, that one joint of our finger might shine againe … savage beasts (I well thinke) ward and save her, they keep sacrilegious hands from doing her injurie." [1]

Pliny the Elder, 23–79 CE

The Historie of the World
(alternatively known as
Natural History)

INTRODUCTION

G ems and minerals have always been a source of fascination. Kings, queens, pharaohs, oracles, priestesses, priests, and wisdom keepers from all spiritual paths have adorned themselves with and/or been buried with them. These gemstones help connect them to power, privilege, spiritual wisdom, and protection and ensure safe passage to the majestic palaces of the afterlife. Battle breastplates and belts of Roman warriors held gemstones bezel set in shining metal—certain crystals, including topaz, to protect them; others, such as chrysoberyl, to make them invisible to their enemies. Queens from every monarchy, their crowns often bejeweled with diamonds for longevity and rubies for power, assume an otherworldly, divine right authority when wearing their royal jewels. Brides often wear a single, round, white diamond before they receive and accept the marital band. Gemstone carvings are found in nearly every burial site of significance around the world, from ancient Sumer to modern monarchies.

Why? Perhaps on some level there is universal recognition crystals could represent a code, a hidden language of stored and embedded wisdom reflecting the state of our planet at the time of their formation. Such a code could even be an unspoken language among humans—conscious or subconscious. The colors, markings, mining locations, and energies of our crystals are like dialects of a sacred language we are all still learning, hints and secrets of times past.

Even beyond their meaning, we must consider the beauty of gemstones. Human beings are conditioned to appreciate beauty, symmetry, balance, and simplicity; aesthetically, these qualities please the human eye most. Crystals grow in specific and unique molecular structures, and each structure offers a unique balance and play of light, like a fingerprint. Yes, crystals are Gaia's beautiful, divine fingerprints. They tell you she was here, and she has wisdom to share with her children.

Something magical happens when you hold a crystal or slip on a jewel-encrusted ring. The crystal's energy fuses with your energy field. Suddenly you feel grounded and safe as you gaze into the deep, blood-red Indian garnet's glow, or come into a deep sense of calm when you look down into the facets of a brilliant-cut African amethyst, glimmers of burgundy and hints of bright orange glowing from its fiery depths. Our ancestors did not resist these crystal enchantments; rather, they learned to appreciate and seek the wisdom of the mineral kingdom by carrying and wearing prized, specialty-cut gemstones from around the world. Their fascination with crystals might be why we had such profoundly successful early trade routes from Africa through Asia and as far north as the remote Himalayas of Tibet. Gemstones, much like herbs and spices, were traded and sought after by monarchs and common people from all walks of life. No mortal could resist the call of the glimmering jewels mined from deep within Gaia's bountiful belly. The longer their route to market, the more precious and desired they became. After all, humans have always most desired the things farthest from their reach.

But human interest in crystals has not been driven by rarity alone. Crystals each have a unique energetic vibration, as all matter does—a cosmic imprint sensitive beings can translate and understand. For example, Cleopatra may have intuitively sensed lapis lazuli was uniquely powerful. Perhaps that is why she initiated long-distance trade for it from remote regions of Afghanistan direct to her palace. Lapis lazuli has been mined continuously for thousands of years in northern Afghanistan, and, even today, Afghan sources provide the highest quality lapis lazuli in the world.

Cleopatra secured most available sources of lapis during her rule and had the walls of her palace inlaid with the deep-blue stone. She ground it into powder and lined her eyes with it, believing the blue color enhanced both her personal power and her intuition. She may have learned of its power-bearing reputation from legends of her predecessor, Queen Puabi of Sumeria. In the ancient Sumerian tombs of Ur located underneath modern-day Baghdad, thousands of ornate lapis carvings were found alongside graves and mummified remains. In fact, Queen Puabi's seal was found at her gravesite, carved into a lapis stamp wheel; it is now

> Gemstones are timekeepers and record holders of an ancient wisdom helping you lead a more meaningful, powerful, prosperous, and intentional life.

housed at the British Museum. The lapis seal of Puabi dates to 2600 BCE, predating Cleopatra's reign by more than 2,000 years.

While *lapis lazuli* may simply mean "blue stone," it is much more than just a blue gem. Lapis lazuli is the currency of queens. Even modern prophets and psychics, such as Edgar Cayce, have credited lapis (as well as other gems from the region, including azurite) with increased access to higher levels of conscious awareness.

Indeed, crystal legends, lore, and myths open you to a powerful and magical lineage you may have never been exposed to and it is, indeed, your lineage. Once you learn the legends, you understand why humans have been intrigued by crystals for millennia, traveling many miles to acquire, and then insisting on being buried with, their treasures. No matter how far back into history you search or how far across our planet you travel, you find endless evidence of ancient and modern significance attributed to gemstones. This book is a modern attempt to curate and weave those stories and narratives into a comprehensive, accurate account of how we came to view our gemstones the way we do today.

Whether you are new to gemstones and crystals, or you have been an avid collector and student for years, this book will have something to capture your attention and interest. No matter your age, and no matter how much you know, you never lose your appetite for new wisdom or your desire for a compelling story. We are hardwired to appreciate the past in service of understanding the present and predicting the future.

And that is what gemstones are—the past, eternalized and crystallized into a form you can hold in your hand today. They are timekeepers and record holders of an ancient wisdom helping you lead a more meaningful, powerful, prosperous, and intentional life. As they formed in our Earth over thousands—even millions—of years, they literally crystallized the knowledge of our planet and what was happening as they formed. Crystals arrest time. The ancient Lemurians knew well that gemstones, in particular quartz crystals, were easily programmed to hold, send, and receive information. Perhaps that is why Lemurian elders and priests encoded and encrypted their wisdom and their ways into the Lemurian seed crystals. They set an intention—once human civilization was ready to return to the Lemurian ideals of universal love and united consciousness, the seed crystals could release their stored wisdom to those light bearers ready to receive and transmit it. Those transmissions

are occurring today, connecting healers who share Lemurian roots across space and time. Every stone creates and shares unique transmissions, a rainbow of light spread across Earth in layers of crystallized time.

Just how many crystals are there on Earth right now? According to the Mineralogical Society of America, there are about 3,800 known and identified minerals on the planet today. On average, thirty to fifty new minerals are identified, and several are discredited, each year. New mineral inclusions identified within well-known minerals such as quartz allow for entirely new variations of common minerals to be mined and researched each year.

And, of course, the same mineral can grow in two different locations and look quite different as a result. Uruguayan amethyst and Brazilian amethyst are a great example: Both are beautiful purple amethyst stones, but Uruguay is home to a lot of stalactite formations that yield round flower-shaped slices of amethyst crystals in deeper hues and exotic colors like rose-pink. Meanwhile in Brazil, you find light-colored amethyst specimens without as much stalactite activity. Same stone, different location, and, thus, a different appearance, growth structure, energy, and price point. Indeed, part of the mystery underscoring our appreciation of gemstones lies in different locations on Earth where they are mined. This book refers to ancient ley lines and points of historical and energetic significance, often called vortex points, to understand how a crystal's geographic location affects its energy and application. Practitioners in the metaphysical realm know these lines and points as Earth's crystalline grid.

When it comes to gemstones, size, location, quality, clarity, history, weather patterns, and, of course color and cut matter. This comprehensive review of modern and ancient gemstone legends and lore takes you back as far as ancient Lemuria, before exploring modern geological history to understand the recent rise in popularity of magical meteoritic glass from Siberia and Egypt, the result of extraterrestrial collisions with Earth as long ago as twenty to thirty million years. With the rise of modern Greek and Roman civilizations came efforts to find utilitarian purposes for crystals and minerals; the development of the mining industry as a global source of trade activity brought wisdom about the relationship between certain minerals and metals. The concept of gemstones and crystals as valuable "ore" materials of more commonly available minerals such as manganese helped fuel economies, and even supported advancements in wellness, throughout parts of the world.

Modern medicine and dentistry turned to the mineral kingdom for critical health and wellness discoveries in recent centuries: fluorite brought fluoride for dental health; lepidolite (micanized lithium) became a potent treatment for bipolar disorder; zircon yielded zirconium compounds for deodorant; and halite became table salt. Modern esoteric movements shifted the focus in the later part of the twentieth century from the medicinal and practical uses of crystals to their magical and metaphysical properties. From the father of ancient geology, Damigeron, and his seminal work *De Virtutibus Lapidum* or *The Virtues of Stones*, to more modern sources like George Frederick Kunz's *The Curious Lore of Precious Stones* and Judy Hall's *The Crystal Bible*, we can gather a general understanding of how crystals developed their metaphysical reputations and commonly accepted uses. In addition, ritual, practical, ceremonial, royal, and spiritual uses of gemstones and minerals are explored with the goal of offering as comprehensive a timeline and encyclopedia of crystal history as possible.

And to be sure, it's a legendary history full of lavish tales of secret wisdom, dark magic, miraculous healing, royal intrigue, and extraterrestrial influences. Oh yes, stories of alien encounters, spontaneous healing, and mysterious manifestation are woven into the fabric of the world's historical crystal legends! Stories are the way we understand ourselves, our history, our modern world, and what the future holds. Through stories we come to understand our own undeniable fascination with crystals and their wisdom. As you read each story offered here, apply your personal filter, that of your history and evolution, your lineage. See what resonant stories and experiences surface within you that offer insight into your journey with crystals and gems. Maybe you had a past life in ancient Atlantis or Egypt, and that is why you are so called to those geographies in this lifetime, or perhaps it is why you feel your pulse quicken when you hold a piece of Larimar from the Dominican Republic—Atlantis is rising in your hand. Gemstones are transmitters of light, time, and wisdom. If you think about their growth process, they are keepers and translators of seismic and geographic activity. Begin to view your crystals as teachers, and the entire mineral kingdom becomes a fertile classroom.

Many people use the terms *crystal, gemstone,* and *mineral* interchangeably, especially in metaphysical contexts. As is common in metaphysical contexts, this book will use the terms *gemstones, gems,* and *crystals* interchangeably to denote a naturally occurring material with rare properties, such as color or clarity, offering special energetic or monetary value. In most cases, gemstones are crystals, with unique repeating crystalline structures. While some gems are not crystals and are, in fact, organic material, such as opals or obsidian (considered amorphous crystals by most geologists), these are exceptions to the general rule and, as such, will not be discussed using other terminology to avoid confusion.

The word *crystal* is derived from the Greek word *krystallos*, meaning "ice"; our ancient ancestors believed all quartz crystals were actually ancient forms of solidified water. Today we know crystals are not frozen water, but the term *crystal* remains as part of our standard lexicon in the gem and mineral industry.

This book approaches crystal legends and myths through an historical lens and is organized chronologically, anchoring the journey in seminal moments, contexts, and civilizations in which gemstones played important roles. Chapter 1 takes us as far back in time as we can go in metaphysical terms, to understand the first "mother" civilizations of Mu, or Lemuria, and Atlantis. Mu was the cradle of the first species on our planet, the Lemurians, who lived and thrived in the South Pacific thousands of years ago. On the opposite side of the globe was Atlantis, anchored firmly in the Atlantic Ocean, where the Atlantean civilization rose and cultivated technical and technological expertise. The priests and priestesses of Lemuria and Atlantis were transported to other geographical locations, or vortex points, around the Earth when their civilizations were submerged and destroyed. Some went within the Earth to escape, recover, and rebuild while others traveled to India, Egypt, and other remote locations to commence new paradigms of existence. Thoth, an Atlantean priest, went to Egypt, where he launched the ancient Egyptian empire and organized its pantheon of gods.

Thus, chapter 2 explores Egyptian and Mesopotamian use of crystals and the integration of gemstones into their mythology. Chapter 3 turns farther east to India, where gems were thought to be offerings to the gods and goddesses, sacred to the forces of all creation. Here there is a discussion of the role of gemstones and crystals in the development of modern astrology. Chapter 4 traces early Egyptian and Indian influences to Rome and Greece, exploring the role of crystals and gems in these powerful empires. Chapter 5 explores Christian biblical references to gemstones, which, in many ways, is an integration of early Egyptian and Indian wisdom. In chapter 6, the regal history of crystals and gems is unearthed to show how European kings and queens used gemstones to ensure power, divine right authority, and longevity. Chapter 7 discusses crystals and much more modern discoveries used by crystal healers and light workers today. And finally, chapter 8 covers crystals associated with the Western Zodiac.

Indeed, modern traditions suggest crystals are Earth's exoskeleton, each bone connected to all others by space and time, and each gemstone encodes access to the grand mystery of life. Unlocking these codes and putting the puzzle pieces together can bring healing on all levels—

physical, mental, and emotional. Through a focus on healing, crystals are experiencing a renaissance. The history of gemstones is always evolving; parts of the old stories re-written as modern audiences integrate their wisdom and experiences into narratives of the past. The conclusion offers a chance for the gemstones discussed in this book to speak directly to you and offer their specific channeled wisdom as a form of sacred meditation with the crystal kingdom. What would your crystals say to you, each from their unique vantage points, if they could speak?

The goal of this book is a lofty one—to bring the history of gemstones and crystals to life in a way that honors the magic and mystery of a three-thousand-plus years-long romance with gems. While most of the stories are as old as the Egyptian desert and many lack an anchor in verifiable fact or physical evidence, they have been told and retold for centuries and are now part of the fabric of our understanding of our world, its creation, its evolution, and, in modern times, its ascension.

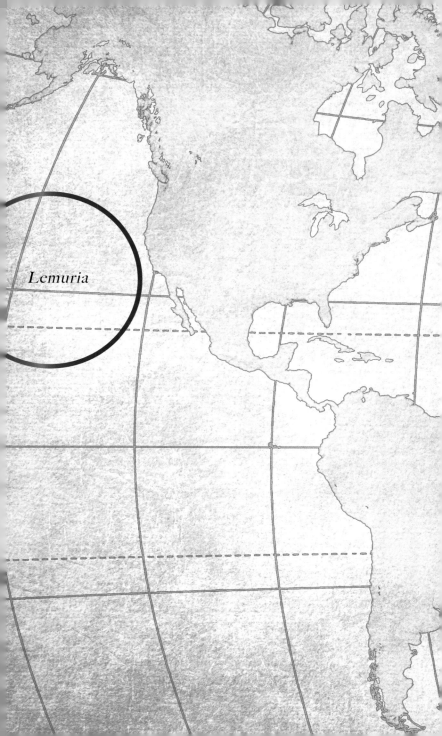

Chapter 1

CRYSTALS OF
ATLANTIS AND LEMURIA

Atlantis and Lemuria live in the realm of legend rather than history. We have little proof of their existence beyond the famed Naacal tablets and vast networks of mysteriously etched crystals; many claim they contain the encoded wisdom of these rumored civilizations. Plato referred to Atlantis in two of his Socratic dialogues. The story recounts an ancient civilization, a utopia of sorts, destroyed by floods. Recent discoveries of large sunken landmasses may hold keys to the mysteries. But even in the absence of scientific proof, many believe human life traces its origins to Lemuria, also known as *Mu* or the "mother" civilization.

More than 100,000 years ago, a galactic alliance of star beings volunteered to launch a lineage of human inhabitants on a new planet, Earth, to perpetuate peace and light in a new part of the galaxy. Lemuria sat on a giant landmass between what is now California and Australia, with the heart, or center, on the island of Mu, where Kauai is today. Deeply intuitive visitors to Hawaii say they can feel the energy of Lemuria rising there. Lemuria began as a grand experiment to anchor higher-dimensional star energies in third-dimensional human systems. Lemurian beings came primarily from Sirius and the Pleiades, which are stars aligned to energies of love, peace, and Christ consciousness; in fact, Sirius is believed to be the star the Magi followed to find Christ after his birth.

Lemurian beings were taught to activate the seven *chakras*, or energy centers in the human system, tethering them to Earth's crystalline grid via the earth star chakra and aligning them to the broader cosmic gateways via the soul star chakra. In this way, a direct line of energy extended from the first-dimensional crystalline core of the planet through the *sushumna*, or energetic column, in the physical body all the way to the ninth-dimensional stargates and beyond. This energy line became an open channel through which information could be received, stored, and transmitted.

Such an energy line required a natural source of power. Earth was chosen for Lemurian colonization because it is rich in silicon dioxide, or quartz crystals, which can be used to raise and attune human frequency, transmit energy, and send and receive information from higher dimensions. Thus, Lemurians could take on physical form and still access a full range of extrasensory data. They learned to program information into quartz, and, for this reason, we have access to much of their advanced wisdom when we work and meditate with Lemurian quartz; by running your fingertip along the ridges, or "stairway to heaven," on alternating sides of Lemurian quartz crystals, you activate and can channel whatever wisdom is stored within your piece.

While some say Lemurians scrambled to seed their wisdom into quartz when they learned of their doomed fate, a more likely scenario is they were working with quartz all along. Lemurians intuitively understood how to work with Earth's crystalline grid to remain in third-dimensional reality and, yet, still activate higher dimensional doors of perception. The pineal gland within the human brain connected to quartz crystals like transmitters—channeling and sending information across dimensions, even if the human being was unaware this was happening. Crystal healers continue to work with quartz as a transmitter today, opening their chakras and energetic access points to receive information, send healing, and transmute lower vibrations. Those attracted to quartz are said to remember when quartz was much more than just a rock, but a key that unlocked many doors of awareness.

The Lemurian age was largely one of undisturbed peace—a kind of heaven on Earth, one that enjoyed relative harmony for thousands of years. Disruption came when a vastly different species—the Annunaki— arrived from their home planet of Nibiru in search of gold, which Earth held in impressive supply. Nibiru was warming at an unprecedented rate, and gold molecules could be used to repair the shield of its outermost atmosphere. When the Annunaki arrived, they colonized land on the other side of the world from Lemuria and began to source gold in steady supply; however, the Annunaki soon realized it was an arduous task to mine gold from Earth's multi-layered surface. They set out to create their own human race—to mine gold as quickly and efficiently as possible. Lemurian beings were gentle, loving, and kind, so the community they formed held that pure vibration of loving kindness. The Annunaki were different; they embodied a lower, more materialistic vibration, focusing their efforts not on expansion of consciousness but on access to resources acquired through serial fragmentation of collective awareness.

The race of beings the Annunaki propagated were the Atlanteans, who were endowed with technological and physical prowess, making them ideal workers, scientists, and engineers. If Lemurians were the divine feminine emerging on Earth, Atlanteans were the divine masculine. Soon, there was no balance between the two and incessant fighting began—fighting that would lead to mutual destruction and ritual purification of the planet. The Annunaki were said to be fascinated by human women. In fact, some believe ancient Sumerians were a hybrid Atlantean human race, which would explain their rapid advancement and technological sophistication. The Annunaki lust for power, money, knowledge, and resources quickly downshifted Earth's overall frequency. Peaceful angelic Lemurians found themselves in conflict with materialistic, transactional Atlanteans—and both experienced a premonition of their mutual demise. The Lemurians encoded final wisdom into their beloved quartz crystals and safeguarded them in key locations where they could be mined thousands of years later by those prepared to work with Lemurian lineage, once again activating their wisdom on Earth. Metaphysical practitioners believe the discovery of Lemurian crystals in Brazil in 1999 signaled the dawn of the Age of Aquarius and human ascension.

Reasons for the destruction of Atlantean and Lemurian civilizations, via what is known as the Grand Flood or The Deluge, are unclear, but the Annunaki home planet of Nibiru may have collided with Earth, causing a shift of poles and floods that led to tsunamis, engulfing major landmasses. Most major religious traditions, including Christian and Mayan sacred texts, refer to a great flood that destroyed most of Earth's surface and living inhabitants in ancient times. Anywhere from 60 to 90 percent of Earth's population may have perished by drowning. Metaphysicians maintain the ongoing conflict between masculine and feminine forces led to the planet's ritual purification by flood.

Lemurians who survived the flood fled west, but Atlanteans largely fled east, with the most famous Atlantean—their priest, Thoth—escaping to Egypt. Thoth transferred knowledge of frequency, vibration, and sound to northern Africa, where he used advanced technologies to move the pyramids into a formation based on precise measurements of his home constellation, the Pleiadian star system. Thoth's mother, Maia, was the oldest of the seven Pleiadian stars. Atlantean beings also fled to Central America and guided the building of the ancient Mayan pyramids there (the Maya are likely named after the Pleiadian star Maia). Others arrived in northeastern Avalon (modern day Glastonbury, England), to honor and perpetuate the goddess aspect of the Atlantean lineage. The scattering of energies sent shock waves into the farthest corners of our universe. In response, a council of higher evolutionary star beings outside Earth's atmosphere created a protective shield around the planet to safeguard humans from outside detection and influence; this shield also prevented humans from accessing greater dimensional awareness and, thus, resulted in a dramatic loss of insight, intuition, and magic. Such is the price we pay today for relative safety in our galaxy—we have difficulty seeing the star beings now, and they have difficulty reaching us. Some refer to this shield as the Galactic Wall and suggest crystals are capable of piercing the wall, channeling and decoding wisdom as well as serving as points of direct contact from the outer realms of our universe.

People drawn to crystals are likely descendants of these early civilizations. Those with clairabilities—clairaudience, clairsentience, and clairvoyance—are said to be awakening now to Lemurian and Atlantean frequencies channeled through the re-emergence of crystals from these ancient civilizations. If you can hear them, they are calling you.

CRYSTAL

Atlantisite

Barite

Heulandite

Lemurian blue calcite

Lemurian seed quartz

Larimar

Scepter quartz

Record keeper crystals

CRYSTALS OF ATLANTIS AND LEMURIA AT A GLANCE

PROPERTIES	PLACE OF ORIGIN (Ancient and Modern)
associated with Atlantis and Lemuria; helps form and strengthen existing psychic boundaries to protect empaths from burnout and psychic attack	Tasmania
associated with Atlantis; instant manifestation of thought into form, higher dimensional awareness	Morocco, India, China, Mexico, Africa, United States
associated with Atlantis; facilitates higher awareness and heart chakra awakening, balance between emotional and intellectual energies	India
associated with Lemuria; water and Earth energies; connection to high altitude and pyramid building as well as interdimensional communication	Argentina
associated with Lemuria; encoded crystals infused with the wisdom of Lemuria and the disembodied experience of consciousness, higher awareness	Brazil
associated with Atlantis; water energy, connection to dolphin magic and extrasensory awareness, multiple forms of communication, intuition	Dominican Republic
associated with Lemuria; considered the wands of high priests and priestesses; able to direct massive waves of energy between dimensions of reality	Brazil
associated with Atlantis; trifold law of three, accredited to Thoth and his teachings, rise of mathematics, and sacred geometry	Brazil

ATLANTISITE

Atlantisite with stichtite is a rare, desirable crystal found exclusively in Tasmania. Sought by healers and empaths to help them establish healthy spiritual and psychological boundaries, Atlantisite is also known to open channels to ancient Atlantean wisdom. Atlantisite promotes healthy energetic boundaries by dissolving ancient energetic blockages and repairing energetic channels. It activates and purifies the Kundalini, or life force energy, while it removes debris from the *subtle body*, another name for the energetic field around the human body.

Because it activates and purifies at the same time, Atlantisite lets you safely open your energetic field and become a clear channel while you purify the energies flowing through you. In this way, you are able to channel, transmit, and filter energy all at once—keeping good energy in and letting bad energy go.

Atlantisite also activates deep cellular memory, an important tool in the physical and energetic healing process. Empaths use Atlantisite to avoid taking on their clients' health challenges and emotional issues. Its energy helps you stay out of the pathway of healing and purification, maintaining your personal energetic perimeters. Atlantisite reminds healers that healing work is done *through* them, not *because* of them. Bypassing the human capacity to heal and working directly with source energy, Atlantisite accelerates quantum healing by tapping into the highest possible frequencies of light not normally accessible in the human 3D realm.

Just as Atlantean beings were concerned with technology and advancement, this crystal seeks the clearest path to higher evolutions of healing frequencies, which makes it ideal for anyone struggling with serious and persistent health issues.

BARITE

Barite as a mineral is extremely heavy; in fact, its name comes from the Greek word *barys*, meaning "heavy." Barite comes in a variety of colors, from gray to green to gold, and is largely associated with Atlantis. Barite facilitates instant manifestation of thought into form, crystallizing consciousness. Found in many countries around the world including Morocco, Mexico, and the United States, barite is relatively accessible on the mineral market. In 2015, computer scientist Michael Hubner located what he believed was the epicenter of the lost Atlantean continent, on the edge of the Moroccan coast. Using fifty-one clues left behind by Greek philosopher Plato in his ancient descriptions of Atlantis in *Timaeus* and *Critias*, written more than two thousand years ago, Hubner entered all possible data points into his computer program and determined the Souss-Massa region was the final resting place (above sea level) of Atlantis.

Within Souss-Massa is a sacred national park, and nearby ancient libraries contain records of significance about mathematics, geometry, the use of medicinal plants, astronomy, and more. Crystals from the Moroccan region carry a mystical, vibrant, expansive energy that heals by supporting the soul's highest purpose and an inclusive awareness of soul purpose.

Barite clears blockages in the upper chakras including karmic debt from misuse of psychic gifts in previous or current lifetimes, before access to higher levels of conscious awareness. Atlantis was the ancient civilization where power first became abused, and lineages of abuse of power continue today; these lineages can be purified and cleared with barite.

HEULANDITE

While the Atlanteans were largely concerned with technological and scientific advancement, they also worked important love magic and were concerned with the process of heart opening as a tool for human and spiritual advancement. Heulandite is one of the crystal keys capable of unlocking the mysteries and wisdom of the Atlantean root race. Heulandite comes primarily in two shades—pink and green—both of which open the heart chakra.

Green heulandite is a master healer of the subtle body. Disease first begins as an energetic disturbance in the subtle body before it manifests in the physical body; by working with heulandite, you can discern the early signs of disease and illness in your body or that of your client. Placing heulandite over the heart chakra opens you to love from all directions, allowing you to receive love openly and graciously, which helps you attract even more love into your life. Heulandite also unlocks keys to understanding your love contracts in this lifetime, both with those you currently have relationships with and those you might meet and love in the future.

You can meditate with heulandite to heal karmic bonds related to emotional wounds, such as betrayal, abandonment, and dishonesty so they can be released and not continue to manifest in the form of dysfunctional relationships.

LEMURIAN
BLUE CALCITE

A new light blue calcite was found in 2010 in Argentina. Called Lemurian blue or aquatine calcite in the marketplace, it carries a Lemurian vibration. Found at a 15,000-foot (4.5 km) elevation, Lemurian blue calcite carries ascension energies and a strong vibrational connection to the source.

Calcite, in general, is associated with happiness and peace. Lemurian blue calcite is a strong water element stone that allows for opening of the heart and throat chakras, reminding you of your healing power and lineage. It can attract higher-order angels to protect you during times of difficulty. In metaphysical circles, Lemurian blue calcite is said to help unlock past-life memories of Lemurian lifetimes, accessing wisdom and healing codes you still carry from those lives. By meditating with Lemurian blue calcite, you connect both with ancient wisdom and extra-dimensional awareness, anchoring the past and the future in the present moment. When you bring your past and future healing gifts together in service of your current work, you expand your repertoire of wisdom and tools. The longer you work with this—and any Lemurian crystal—the more likely you are to download wisdom from relevant lifetimes there. Hold Lemurian blue to your throat chakra to help you explore your deepest truth and purpose for incarnating in the current lifetime, especially if confused or you find yourself at a turning point right now.

LEMURIAN
SEED QUARTZ CRYSTALS

Perhaps the most famous of all Lemurian crystals are Lemurian seed crystals, implanted with wisdom by Lemurian high priests and priestesses set to be activated long after their civilization's doomed fate. Thousands of tales tell the story of the high priests and priestesses spending ample time encoding secret messages and accelerated wisdom into the lines and markings of each crystal. These pieces were then dispatched to locations around the world, most notably to Minas Gerais, Brazil, where most of today's Lemurian quartz crystals are found and mined. A very small number of quartz points were also encoded with trigons—raised or etched perfect triangles—on the faces (discussed on page 33). All Lemurian seed crystals are master healers, but each is designed and encoded to heal a unique system, either the physical or subtle body of the one who finds it. Lemurian seed crystals are characterized by raised horizontal lines across alternate surfaces, though some do not hold to this alternating pattern.

To meditate with and download wisdom from your Lemurian seed crystal, hold the crystal in your receptive (for most people, the right or writing) hand and close your eyes. Run your fingertips over the horizontal lines, referred to as the "stairway to heaven" in metaphysical circles, beginning at the base of the crystal and working your way to the tip. Once you reach the last line, keep your finger or thumb there and focus your third eye on any visions that emerge. At the last line of encoded wisdom, new levels of wisdom are activated—every time you meditate. For this reason, Lemurian seed crystals like to develop a lifelong relationship with their owner, revealing new pieces of their destiny or soul path each time their crystal wisdom is sought and activated.

If possible, keep all Lemurian crystals you own for the duration of your life. They are lifelong teachers that activate wisdom when appropriate and needed; you are unlikely to be finished with them or their wisdom in one lifetime. A rare form of Lemurian quartz called Lemurian root quartz is found under Lemurian crystals in Brazil and is considered a storehouse of the deepest secrets from the Lemurian civilization. Lemurian root crystals are rare and difficult to find in the marketplace today, but may contain additional light codes for healing and transformation not yet discovered or activated.

LARIMAR

Larimar is a beautiful robin's egg blue crystal found only in mines surrounding the Dominican Republic—a gloriously beautiful Caribbean island whose waters are crystal clear and full of tropical sea life. In 1916, Father Miguel Domingo Fuertes Lorén first discovered a piece of Larimar there. Word reached Edgar Cayce, famed clairvoyant and channel, who thereafter referred to Larimar as the "rare blue stone of Atlantis." Even today many refer to Larimar as "Atlantis stone." Early pieces of Larimar were found atop the sands of Dominican beach shoreline, but then seemed to disappear—until 1974, when a Dominican named Miguel Mendez ventured upstream in search of additional sources of the curious blue crystal. He requested permission from the Dominican government to continue mining, and so, to this day, we enjoy a steady but limited supply of this mystical stone. Mendez named the stone for his daughter, Larissa, and the word *mar*, meaning "ocean" in Spanish. Larimar has never been found outside the Dominican Republic. Its crystal wisdom is truth—the telling and the knowing of truth—both for others and for oneself. It is a powerful activator of the throat chakra, which is the seat of our human voice. Larimar, in that way, is a potent tool of empowerment and activation of divine wisdom as translated through us.

SCEPTER CRYSTALS

According to legend, scepter crystals were placed atop the magical wands of the highest order of Lemurian priests and priestesses. Scepters form when one crystal begins to grow over another, creating a crystal crown. This rare formation creates a wand—a powerful tool of instantaneous or quantum manifestation. Scepters are found in clear quartz, smoky quartz, elestial quartz, amethyst, and, in rare cases, citrine.

Lemuria and Atlantis were mystery schools experimenting in the raising, managing, and transmuting of energies across multiple dimensions. Scepters were their magical wands—the most potent form of quartz—because they contain not just one termination on each end, but two; one encased over the other. This sheath-like shape not only magnified the potency of the scepter wand's energy but also allowed Lemurians to perform healing ceremonies and psychic surgeries to remove unwanted or unneeded energies in the auric field. Lemurian high priests and priestesses also used scepters to direct and raise energy for expansion of collective consciousness. To ensure a legacy of wisdom and magic, Lemurian leaders used scepters to encode their wisdom into Lemurian points and clusters; the lines of Lemurian crystals are said to be etched *only* by scepter points.

When you want to grow or expand something, meditate on your desire and then use a scepter wand to direct energy toward it; you will experience double the manifestation in half the time—a gift of accelerated development and creation from the Lemurian elite.

RECORD KEEPER CRYSTALS

Record keepers are raised or indented trigons (raised or etched perfect triangles) found on the face of rare crystals from the Atlantean root race. Occasionally, record keepers are found in holographic form and can be seen within a crystal but are neither raised nor indented; in holographic form, trigons often appear not as a single, or even double, marking but in rows of what can look like hundreds, if not thousands, of tiny prismatic triangles. While some Lemurian seed crystals are trigonic, meaning they contain record keepers, most are not.

Record keepers have been found on the faces of amethyst crystals, Herkimer diamonds from New York, rubies and sapphires from India and Burma, and aquamarine from Afghanistan. To determine if your crystal contains a record keeper, scan all surfaces of the crystal in bright, clear, reflective light. If you locate a triangle, you are in luck. Once you identify the triangle, focus your vision on it, anchoring your vision in the three points. Every trigon bears three main energy streams, or pieces of embodied wisdom, for the one who discovers it. By meditating with your record keeper crystal and asking your guides to reveal your three pieces of encrypted wisdom, you will access your unique stored wisdom—wisdom you can use to grow, develop, and improve your life.

In ancient alchemical traditions, the triangle was the center of all power symbols created to represent the sacred art of transmutation—changing base materials to gold. Perhaps this is why our ancient ancestors preferred to build pyramids as temples, honoring the historical significance of the number three and the shape of the triangle, which raises Earth's energy skyward, manifesting the hermetic principle, "As above, so below," in material form. The number three is sacred in almost every magic, spiritual, and theological tradition, including the Christian tradition, in which God is said to inhabit three distinct aspects: the Father, the Son, and the Holy Spirit. The divine feminine represents three separate life phases—the maiden, the mother, and the crone. Saturn divides the human life cycle into three "returns," in which life lessons are learned in repeating cycles, each an opportunity for renewal, purification, and redemption. Consider the record keeper a reminder of your personal cycles and unique evolution toward your soul's fullest potential.

ACCESSING CRYSTAL WISDOM: ATLANTIS AND LEMURIA

If you wish to connect to the crystalline wisdom of Atlantis and Lemuria, choose two crystals from these magical civilizations and hold one in each hand. Then, imagine that your soul is able to travel back in time to its earliest incarnation, perhaps as a Lemurian or Atlantean priest or priestess when you would have been present to the frequencies of this time. What wisdom would have been available to you and how would you have activated its power? What wisdom can you glean from these crystals now in present time?

ATLANTISITE

Atlantisite is a **boundary keeper**, a crystal that keeps the bad out and the good in. For empaths, Atlantisite is a potent crystal ally that immediately and intuitively guards the auric field. Hold Atlantisite in your nonwriting, projecting, hand to project energies of balance and protection; hold Atlantisite in your writing, or receiving, hand to call in tighter boundaries and prevent energy slippage through hidden leaks in your energy field.

BARITE

Barite is a **purifier of karmic debt** and **karmic wounds**, allowing you to purify the past, present, and future. Hold barite in your nonwriting, projecting, hand and visualize sending these energies of purification and clearing down both the maternal and paternal lines of your family lineage. Then, hold barite in your writing, or receiving, hand to receive purification energies gently releasing anything that no longer serves you.

HEULANDITE

Heulandite is attuned to the broader **heart chakra frequency of our planet**. It is a **supreme stone of love attraction**, helping you call in love from all directions. Meditate by placing a piece of green or pink heulandite on your heart and imagine that light radiating from your heart, out across the universe, sending and receiving heart-healing frequencies to support your growth and development.

LEMURIAN BLUE CALCITE

Lemurian blue calcite **opens gateways to higher truth**, allowing you to hear the voice of your higher self. It also lets you access the planetary crystal grid to align your personal energetic frequency with the higher frequencies of our planet and universe, bringing you into perfect and pure alignment with the highest intention of healers on our planet and spirit guides leading us toward a higher level of cosmic awareness.

LEMURIAN SEED CRYSTALS

Lemurian seed crystals **expand consciousness**. Lemurian seed and root crystals are the **master teachers** in the mineral kingdom and anchor our planet's universal light grid. Call upon them to advance your personal learning and accelerate our planet's ascension. They help guide us toward the next evolutionary stage of our advancement.

LARIMAR

Larimar is a healer of the emotional and endocrine systems, facilitating rapid **integration of soul fragments**, or pieces of the soul lost during traumatic human life events. Larimar helps you understand your soul's deepest purpose for being at this time. Place Larimar on your throat chakra to expand your center of personal truth, helping you articulate your needs and desires to those who need to hear them.

SCEPTER QUARTZ CRYSTALS

Scepters are the **original magic wands of our universe**. Within each of us, queen and king energies lie dormant, awaiting our maturity and sovereignty. Scepter crystals raise your inner queen or king, summoning your deepest inner authority and reminding you that you need no one's permission to manifest your highest purpose. You have had the magic within you all along.

RECORD KEEPER CRYSTALS

Record keeper crystals remind you of the vast power of the universe and the relationship between thought and form. All manifestation begins with vision and requires sacred geometry to form the basic building blocks of matter. Record keepers **harness the sacred energy of three** and the tri-fold power of source energy in its many incarnations. Meditate on these triangular forms to download sacred wisdom and fast-track your personal integration of spiritual wisdom.

Chapter 2

CRYSTALS OF EGYPT AND MESOPOTAMIA

The earliest recorded human experiences with crystals begin in ancient Mesopotamia, in the birthplace of civilization known as Sumer, located near modern-day Baghdad, Iraq. Sumer brought the first city, Uruk, and temples, called ziggurats, to the world. It also saw the rise of the first queen, Puabi, and first goddess ever worshipped, Inanna. Yes, Sumer was a matriarchy, even though she had kings—including Gilgamesh, fifth king of Uruk. And, even though a seminal poem chronicled his epic life, Inanna endures as the more powerful and revered figure.

CRYSTALS OF EGYPT AND MESOPOTAMIA AT A GLANCE

CRYSTAL	PROPERTIES	PLACE OF ORIGIN (Ancient and Modern)
Chrysocolla	diplomacy, reconciliation, friendship, advocacy	Egypt, Peru
Malachite	physical healing, divine feminine power	Egypt, Afghanistan
Hematite	circulation of energy, physical health, stability, safety	Sumer, Morocco
Garnet	grounding, safety, protection	India, Sumer
Lapis lazuli	power, royal energy	Afghanistan
Emerald	fidelity, power, wisdom, intuition, insight, compassion, new love, eternal love	Egypt, Columbia
Libyan gold tektite	astral travel and interdimensional awareness	Sahara Desert
Tourmaline	divine protection, divine wisdom, love, awareness	Sri Lanka, Afghanistan, Pakistan, Russia, Burma, Untied States, Brazil

The Sumerian civilization existed from roughly 4500 to 2000 BCE. Its earliest forms of communication, called cylinder seals, were often carved from gypsum, a calcium sulfate material. Gypsum is accessible, soft, easy to carve, and able to survive well in dry desert air, and so it was the optimal material for daily use. Cylinder seals were also carved of hematite, one of the most protective minerals in the crystal kingdom. On these seals, our Sumerian ancestors engraved images and words in cuneiform, the first written language, which was a series of etchings or intentional patterns of hatch marks. Sumerian people ascribed properties both to the images on the cylinder seals and the material with which the seal was made.

A person or family's cylinder seal indicated identity, ownership, and station in life; one's seal could also be used to represent images from an important occasion or period, such as a birth, marriage, or death. The seals were used for mundane tasks including sealing bottles or documents, or ceremonially as a rendering of an individual or setting. The seals rolled easily onto wet clay to create tablets, the earliest form of interpersonal written communication. Jewelry was also pressed using the cylinder seal.

The Sumerians also carved ceremonial praying figures from translucent gypsum, sometimes with glimmering golden heads and hand-painted features. Known as votive figures, these were representations of various beings made as offerings in a broad spiritual sense. They were placed in important places, such as temples and ziggurats. Stone was not widely accessible then, so it would have been saved for significant projects, and only the wealthy or powerful would have had access to a personal seal or votive figure.

In ancient times, our ancestors would have wondered why some minerals were only accessible in tiny pockets. Imagine coming across the first gleaming-red almandine crystal in the vast desert. You might think it has unique and even magical properties, and the ground where it was found is also blessed. Stories of its significance would circulate far and wide. You might search for more, and, when only a small amount is found, decide with care what to use it for.

CHRYSOCOLLA

There is no more powerful stone to represent the union of masculine and feminine than chrysocolla. It is, in every sense, the stone of compromise, negotiation, and reconciliation and has been seen and used as such since ancient times. In ancient Egypt, it was called the "wise stone of conciliation," as those who wore it generally arrived at clever comprises when faced with challenges in negotiations. It was also thought chrysocolla protected the wearer against psychological injury, either through psychic attack or emotional abuse. This stone made volatile people more open, patient, and flexible, which is ostensibly why Cleopatra offered chrysocolla beads as a diplomatic gift to visiting officials, delegates, and heads of state.

Chrysocolla was likely first discovered, as most ore minerals are, on the search for the more prized commodity with which it grew—copper. Chrysocolla and malachite (see page 42) are both ores of valuable copper, and, as such, share a mineral composition as well as metaphysical properties rooted in their origin stories. In ancient times, chrysocolla was often confused with turquoise, based simply on appearance, but the two minerals could not be more different. In Israel, small pockets of chrysocolla have grown with malachite and turquoise, and this rare copper ore configuration is referred to in geological circles as Eilat Stone. However, it is more common in Egypt, Afghanistan, and Pakistan to find malachite growing with chrysocolla in an amalgam mineral called malacolla, available in limited supply on the open market today.

What is it about watery chrysocolla that evokes images of union, creation, and harmony? Some say chrysocolla looks like the planet Earth from high above, a replica of Gaia's intricate land and sea patterns, waves of expansive blue and green and every watercolor in between—flowing in and over each other. Indeed, if one could peer inside the womb of the planet, perhaps chrysocolla is what each of us imagines it looks like from above, from inside, from within, and from without. Blue is a calming color that evokes images of the water element, and blue is also the color of sacred truth, aligned to the throat chakra of the ancient Hindu energetic systems. Water is the element of flow, abundance, and creation in feng shui, and water also represents the creative potential of the divine feminine in all her life-giving aspects. Egypt inherited the notion of divine right female authority from Sumer, and, in so doing, also inherited the idea women were innately prepared for leadership, power, and empire building. When a woman today holds chrysocolla and connects to such a potent ancient lineage of possibility and confidence, she, perhaps, retains some connection to a time when her authority would not be questioned. Chrysocolla urges each woman to rise in the tradition of her ancestors who took their rightful place among kings, pharaohs, and wise men as queens, priestess, seers, oracles, and goddesses.

MALACHITE

Certainly Cleopatra would have valued malachite for its healing and diplomatic properties, which could have enhanced her personal and political power. She and many Egyptians prized malachite, from the Greek *malakos*, or "soft," a name derived from its reputation as an ideal carving material.

The hallmark signature of malachite lies in its unique markings—a marbled swirl of concentric rings and round eyes. Some see shifting desert winds and landscapes when they gaze upon the deep green magic of malachite, while others see the planets of the solar system aloft in their heavenly dance, moving in synchronous rhythms—apart yet together. Still others link malachite to the peacock of ancient Greek mythology and Hera, the wife of Zeus, each circle representing one of the eyes of Argus, protecting her from afar. The well-known King Solomon mines along the Red Sea yielded copper and this powerful healing ore, and its uses in ancient times were varied. Many Egyptian tomb paintings reveal malachite powder ground into the paint, but perhaps the most famous Egyptian use of malachite was more superficial in nature— Cleopatra's famous thick green line of malachite eyeliner, thought to ensure her health, longevity, and safety. The use of powdered malachite is discouraged today, as it is known to have toxic properties if inhaled or ingested; and kohl liner, like the ones used in Cleopatra's time, were often made of a galena-based compound containing lead. In ancient times, while mineral makeup was widely used, it could actually have proven dangerous over time to the women wearing it.

From healing to sacred ceremony, from burial practices to immortality rituals, the ancient Egyptians are well known for their appreciation and cultivation of crystal legends, mythology, and tradition. Even now, scientists excavate the Sahara Desert in search of confirmation of the origins of Libyan gold tektite. While Cleopatra serves as a physical anchor for so much of our fascination with ancient Egypt, the roots of her power extend back to ancient Sumer and the origins of matriarchy on our planet that predate her by thousands of years. And though ancient civilizations are often thought of as remedial, parochial, or limited in their knowledge or access to technology, much about Egypt defies logic, reason, or linear timelines of development. Even the creation of the pyramids and their placement, directly mirroring the Pleiadian star constellation, serve as reminders that ancient Egyptians likely had extraterrestrial contact or access to star maps with wisdom and technologies that may exceed what humans can comprehend today. Perhaps some element of that wisdom and heightened awareness remains within stones from this region; maybe Tutankhamun and Cleopatra were aware crystals were actually transmitters of powerful energy, capable of ensuring safe passage of their spirits into the afterlife. What is known without doubt is ancient Egyptians prized their gemstones, carved them with care, and believed they were among the most valuable of all material objects—not only in this lifetime, but in all lifetimes to come.

HEMATITE AND ALMANDINE GARNET

In Sumer, when a sizable garnet was found, it was often carved into talismans and amulets of protection. How our ancestors used their tools was often a function of what they valued or feared most. In Sumer, the predominant fear was of seven evil spirits, called the Utukku, and spells they might cast or curses they might bestow upon the Sumerian people. As a result, any precious stones were used to protect against these dark forces. Hematite and almandine garnet were two gems the Sumerians used to guard against Utukku attack. Hematite, whose name comes from the Greek word *haima*, or "blood," is a potent binder of cosmic energy, helping contain unwanted forces. It facilitates clear circulation of energy in one's energetic field, just as blood circulates freely through the body's venous systems. In that way, hematite can block or prevent energetic or psychic attack, a subject of much interest in Sumer.

Garnet shares the blood red color of hematite crystals and helps ground errant energy, creating a sense of stability and security. Indeed, stories linking hematite and garnet to energies of protection persist today and shape modern metaphysical perspectives on the best gemstones to use for safety, grounding, and stability. Every time a crystal legend is retold, the narrative imprints even more deeply into collective human consciousness.

LAPIS LAZULI

Another favorite crystal among Egyptian queens and pharaohs was lapis lazuli. Its name is a hybrid of the Greek word for "stone," *lapis*, and the Persian word for "blue," *lazhward*. Lapis lazuli's widespread desirability is well documented. The *Epic of Gilgamesh* identifies lapis as a stone for which Sumerians spent years searching. Part of their attraction to lapis lazuli may actually be rooted in confusion between lapis and sapphire, which is what the throne of God in heaven is said to be made from. The tree of knowledge in the Garden of Eden was also said to be carved from a blue gemstone, and its fruit was carved from gemstones representing desired traits or qualities, including those off limits to humans because of their overwhelming power and capacity to manipulate free will. Gilgamesh believed lapis lazuli would ensure his power and longevity, but, in fact, the stone of truth and wisdom he likely sought was actually sapphire. In ancient times, any blue, hard material could have been called lapis lazuli. Ancient people lacked our modern-day ability to distinguish between the different crystal structures that differentiate lapis and the blue mineral corundum (sapphire).[2]

Egyptians may have made a wise mistake in thinking lapis lazuli was sapphire; sapphire would not have been available in good quality or supply during the time of the pharaohs. However, there were large deposits of lapis lazuli in Afghanistan. Cleopatra, during her rule, quarantined most of the available Afghan supply because she believed it was the famed truth stone and brought her not only eternal life but also eternal power. She had her palace walls inlaid in the royal blue stone (lapis lazuli is the reason we have the concept of "royal" blue color today). She even ground lapis into a powder and lined her eyelids with it, symbolizing her truth and power.

Because the word *lazuli*, from its Arabic roots, is also tied to the word *azur*, or "sky," Cleopatra and other Egyptians believed the stone was an amulet that allowed direct communion with sky gods, descendants of ancient Annunaki beings (see chapter 1). Ancient Egyptians were extremely concerned with the afterlife and what tools or amulets might guarantee safe passage from the world of the living to the afterlife and immortal freedom. Cleopatra took advantage of any opportunity to use tools that would support her strength and rise to power both in this lifetime and in the one(s) to follow.

During the European Renaissance, artists ground lapis lazuli to incorporate the rare shade and its powerful energy into famous works of art. Ultramarine pigment, still in use today, was used throughout the Renaissance as the color of choice for skies and oceans. It has appeared in major works of art from Afghan cave art and Indian mural paintings in the sixth and seventh centuries CE to Virgin Mary's robe in a 1640 piece, *The Virgin in Prayer*, by Italian artist Giovanni Battista Salvi da Sassoferrato, to Dutch artist Vermeer's 1665 painting *Girl with a Pearl Earring*.

EMERALD

Egyptian rulers prized emeralds for their perceived powers of wisdom and immortal life. Cleopatra positioned herself as a figure of power and strength, giving great thought to how she presented herself and her country to visitors. As a female ruler at a time when most wars were won by men, she was wise to capitalize on the far-reaching matriarchal roots of the Middle East. After all, Sumer was the first civilization where female mystical and divine power was acknowledged as equal, if not superior, to male strength. Cleopatra used lapis lazuli (see page 46) for expanded internal power, insight, and intuition; she used emerald to create the appearance of *external* power and strength. Emeralds have long held a reputation as a stone of truth and discernment. Cleopatra was attracted to emerald's beauty, its legend as a stone of truth and wisdom, and its relative rarity.

Although Cleopatra may have confused peridot, or green jasper, with emerald, recent sources have confirmed an emerald mine near the Red Sea was operational at the time of her reign.[3] In fact, it was one of the main sources of emeralds until better quality, more abundant supplies were found in Columbia in the sixteenth century; Columbia has been the main supplier of emerald gemstones ever since, with India being second.

Cleopatra also claimed to possess the largest peridot in the world, from Zabargad, which suggests she could tell the difference.

Cleopatra appreciated emeralds not only for their power and their ability to reveal secrets but for their youthfulness and fertility-bringing properties. They were widely associated with spring, rebirth, renewal, growth, and eternal life. She may also have known emerald was one of four stones God gave King Solomon that imbued him with power over all forms of life. Cleopatra would give visiting dignitaries emerald stones carved with her likeness, attaching her visage to arguably the most powerful stone in Egypt and ensuring her reputation as an immortal, omnipotent queen. Even today tales of her love of emeralds are used by salespeople at jewelry boutiques around the world. When Columbian emeralds came to market, the lust for their magic traveled south and, before long, the Incas were using them extensively for adornment and in ceremonial festivities.

Emerald had a reputation in ancient Egypt for dispersing with lies and illusion to connect people with inner truth and ancient wisdom. In Greek mythology, the Emerald Tablet, containing ancient hermetic wisdom, was said to have been found inside a cave, clutched in the skeletal hands of Hermes Trismegistus (Hermes the Thrice-Great). In ancient times, the word was a prized possession. It could not be easily recorded and certainly could not be guaranteed to survive time, weather, or neglect. Consider the value of sacred texts or laws that one priest, ruler, or queen felt could change the lives of their people. How treasured would such an object be, and in whose care would it be left? The writing of a book such as this is proof some of our earlier ancestors were quite successful.

LIBYAN GOLD TEKTITE

The Sumerians birthed a civilization, gave rise to a matriarchy, developed a written language, and cultivated an appreciation for rare gems and minerals they believed were imbued with unique powers, some of which connected them to the gods. These legends were carried to Egypt, where early rulers of that powerful civilization learned of the treasures of the Far East, as well as those that lay waiting within their own lands.

Thirty million years ago, a meteor of substantial size struck Earth close to the surface in the Sahara Desert of eastern Egypt, in what is known as the Great Erg or the sand sea, melting the golden Saharan sand crystals into a material known today as Libyan gold tektite. King Tutankhamun, the young Egyptian pharaoh of the eighteenth dynasty, knew of this material and had it fashioned into amulets during his reign. One particular piece, his breastplate, was located in 1922, although the scarab was not determined to be Libyan tektite until 1998 by Italian mineralogist Vincenzo de Michele.[4] Why would Tutankhamun have placed a carving of this material in the center of his most important ritual and ceremonial possession? It is reasonable to assume it had special powers to him; a king would not leave his afterlife in the hands of just any crystal or gem. The funeral breastplate in ancient Egypt was a form of cosmic life insurance, guaranteeing safe passage to the afterlife and ensuring the weight of the deceased's heart would be lighter than Ma'at's ostrich feather, thus promising eternal life. Because the ziggurats and pyramids of ancient Mesopotamia and Egypt were built with the intention of reaching the sky and communing with the sky gods, some of whom might be considered extraterrestrial light beings in today's metaphysical circles, perhaps the ancient Egyptians sensed the ascension energies in Libyan tektite and appreciated its otherworldly origins for the energy it offered.

Libyan tektite was not identified as such until 1999, and, in March 2006, geologist Farouk El-Baz identified a crater in the Sand Sea area that would have been large enough to serve as evidence of a meteoric collision. As this discovery was being made, a crew of explorers and geologists traveled to the Great Erg to see for themselves how this material gathers along the sand dunes of the Sahara. The trek is long and arduous, and few brave the strong winds to make passage to this remote place. What these scientists found was worthy of their efforts: Small and large pieces of Libyan gold

tektite, or desert glass, strewn openly across 6,500 kilometers (about 4,000 miles) of desert floor; you can simply pick them up with your hands. Yet the climate is inhospitable—no one could physically live there—and the sands shift so frequently the pieces of Libyan gold available and visible today could easily be covered and hidden again within just a few months or years. Perhaps it was this elusive access that captured Tutankhamun's attention all those years ago.

Perhaps Libyan gold tektite and a related material, moldavite (see page 129), are the mysterious and elusive philosopher's stone from the alchemical tradition—a non-earthly substance capable of creating matter from thought. In the Emerald Tablet of Hermes Trismegistus, thought to be the most ancient magical text and foundation of all modern alchemical, spiritual, and magical traditions, clues are given as to the material that can transform base metals to gold or thoughts into form, processes known as alchemy. King Tut's clear appreciation of and faith in this stone are testimony to the possibility that, in Libyan gold, modern crystal healers and practitioners have been given a key to the wisdom of the universe. It is important to recall Thoth is the rumored author of the Emerald Tablet, which is his recounting of wisdom gathered during his time as high priest of Atlantis. Thoth evolved from high priest to a major god in the Egyptian pantheon, credited with the invention of written language—hieroglyphs. It follows that Thoth may have understood the importance of this material, perhaps having witnessed the meteoric collision in the sky, and offered the Emerald Tablet as affirmation to future generations of its value. Today moldavite and Libyan gold tektite are sold as metaphysical tools for interdimensional spiritual access; metaphysical audiences use these crystals for astral travel, as well as channeling, trance, and shamanic journeywork. Once again, the ancient traditions and uses spill over into modern times.

TOURMALINE

As Egyptian legends go, tourmaline formed in the center of the Earth before passing through a rainbow on its way to the Sun, which accounts for its full-spectrum growth patterns in nearly every color. In Egyptian mythology, the Sun is a powerful figure of power and masculine energy. Aligned to the god Ra, the Sun brings life, direction, clarity, and agency. Egyptians worked with tourmaline in its most common colors—pink and green—but also had access to tourmaline in other colors along the spectrum including red (rubellite), golden yellow, brown (dravite), and black (schorl). Later, African and Australian tales of tourmaline's power speak of them as seer stones, capable of helping their bearer predict the future. Even today tourmaline of all colors is believed to protect against black magic and sorcery and open the one who wears or carries it to a higher level of love and universal energy.

Interestingly, the most prolific sources of tourmaline in the early twenty-first century are Afghanistan and Pakistan, where mines are yielding some of the highest quality and most brilliantly clear and colorful tourmaline stones the world has seen. In many ways, the legend of tourmaline is a tale of the differences in energy between East and West, as well as a tale of the integration of those energies, the union of masculine and feminine. Because tourmaline, in its pink and green varieties, represents heart chakra energies of love, compassion, union, and integration, it seems fitting it would be found on opposite sides of the world, embodying in its very form and structure all that divides and all that connects us, on the most fundamental of levels.

ACCESSING CRYSTAL WISDOM:
EGYPT AND MESOPOTAMIA

If you want to work with the magic of the crystals of ancient Egypt and Sumer, gather two to four stones from those identified in this chapter that speak to you. Hold one or two in each hand. Sit comfortably with your legs crossed and your spine straight, bringing your attention to your breath. Allow yourself to journey back in time to those sand-swept lands, all those thousands of years ago. Feel the warmth of the air surrounding you and the fine texture of the sand beneath your bare feet. Turn your face to the Sun, and feel its warm rays soothing every muscle in your body, calling you to relax, soften, and enjoy this experience. Perhaps some of your personal magic still resides in these ancient lands, and now, as the door to the past opens before you, step forward and reclaim this ancient part of yourself. It is time, and you are welcome here.

CHRYSOCOLLA AND MALACHITE

If you have chosen to work with chrysocolla or malachite, focus your attention on the divine feminine energies within you, allowing your entire mind, body, and spirit to soften and allow what is to just be. Remind yourself, you have nothing to fix and nothing to change. All is as it should be. Stake your claim to perfect health with these two crystals, giving thanks for physical and spiritual healing already on its way to you now. Amen, A'ho, so it is.

HEMATITE AND GARNET

If you have chosen to work with garnet or hematite, focus your attention on your blood flowing through your veins, your sacred life force that moves through you effortlessly without your permission or attention. Allow garnet and hematite to remind you all is unfolding in perfect time, and you simply need to be. You are safe, protected, and well. Give thanks for the stability and solidarity of your life in this moment. Amen, A'ho, so it is.

LAPIS LAZULI, EMERALD, AND LIBYAN GOLD TEKTITE

If you have chosen to work with lapis lazuli, emerald, or Libyan gold tektite, recognize you are aligning yourself with the strongest energy streams available in the crystal kingdom from this historical period. The king or queen within you is ready to rise; now is the time to own your authority and take charge of your life. Receive the power of lapis lazuli, the wisdom of emerald, and the interdimensional awareness of Libyan gold tektite. Know you have all the power, wisdom, and awareness you need to manifest the life of your dreams. Focus your vision on what you desire, while giving generous thanks for what you already have. Amen, A'ho, so it is.

TOURMALINE

If you have chosen to work with tourmaline, recognize that you are channeling energies of divine love and discernment. There is no turning back from tourmaline. Whether you work with black tourmaline for divine protection or green tourmaline for divine wisdom, you enter the enchanted realms when you work with tourmaline. It grows in all colors and thus opens all doors to awareness. If tourmaline presents itself to you, the time is right for love and wisdom to enter your life. Celebrate this new phase of growth and, in doing so, you will simultaneously welcome a new era of prosperity. A'ho, so it is.

Chapter 3

CRYSTALS OF INDIA

India has long been—and continues to be—a valued source of minerals and gemstones. Its crystals were first exported via the Silk Road, which led from China through India and Sri Lanka. Romans prized Indian gemstones and traded extensively for them, along with spices such as cardamom and ginger. And in modern metaphysical circles, Indian gems are appreciated because of the energy of India itself, alive with history and a deep spiritual lineage.

India is home to the largest commercial supply of Himalayan quartz. Himalayan quartz is hand-mined instead of machine-mined, and the mines are only accessible by foot—at least a seven-day trek from any paved roads. The Himalayan ridge is usually covered by snow, so the extraction process is dangerous.

H imalayan quartz is considered to possess strong yang energy; the Himalayas are some of the tallest points on Earth, and this masculine Earth energy is both grounding and protective. When Atlantis fell, a brotherhood of high priests fled to Tibet and the Himalayas. There they struck a balance between the conflicting divine masculine and divine feminine energies on the planet. Crystals from Tibet and the Himalayas are considered peacekeeper talismans, with stored wisdom to help manifest global peace and peace within the human heart.

Tibet is widely considered one of the highest vibrational locations on Earth, where the Om vibration, the sound of the name of God, is infused in every aspect of the culture and land. Lemurian legends point to Tibet as the northernmost scattering place of Atlantean priests, a brotherhood of thirteen Atlantean elders who documented and maintained sacred Atlantean codes, practices, and traditions. Tibetan quartz, a carbon and hematite–included variety, transmits sacred healing codes linked to ancient holy traditions. Tibetan quartz is mined at a 15,000-foot (4.5-km) elevation in the Ganesh Himal mountain range bordering Nepal and Tibet. These mines are beyond the reach of traditional machinery, so the crystals must be brought down the mountainside in sacks by hand. Many are *enhydro*, or water filled, with droplets of ancient healing water that can be seen by gently moving the quartz from side to side. Tibetan quartz is the only form of quartz capable of transmuting disease energies because of its high carbon and hematite content; double-terminated Tibetan quartz crystals can be used to remove illness energies from the subtle body using shamanic healing and extraction techniques. It is an especially potent ally in the energetic fight against autoimmune conditions, and it grants permission to manifest one's soul gifts in this lifetime.

India yields her own impressive list of crystals and minerals, including rubies, emeralds, sapphires, and diamonds. And the sacred Ganga and Narmada Rivers yield precious minerals such as the shiva lingam. Shiva lingam are oblong-shaped crystals that wash up along the Narmada River once a year and are said to transmit blessings of spiritual enlightenment, prosperity, and fertility. In traditional shiva lingam, the dark and light shades come together in perfect balance, representing the union of masculine and feminine. Black shiva lingam were especially prized historically; wherever a black shiva was found it was said a temple must be erected. Black shivas represent only a fraction of all shiva lingam, and, in ancient times, no one outside the Hindu temples was able to access them. Even now they are scarce and expensive. The zeolite family of minerals contains six different crystals, some with ties to ancient Atlantis. Apophyllite, the most common and popular of the zeolites, is desired among modern-day mystics for its ability to open the soul star chakra, a gateway to star nations and advanced wisdom.

India was the first country to connect crystal energy to astrology and planetary alignment. This connection originated from the Vedas, ancient and powerful spiritual texts said to be channeled directly from the Akashic records and galactic library. Vedic astrologers established an important connection between the first-dimensional crystalline grid within Earth and the ninth-dimensional astral gateways to other planets in our solar system. By highlighting balance and caution in the use and prescription of gemstones, Vedic astrologers were, in the truest sense, the first crystal healers.

To work with the Navaratna, or nine lucky gems, as a map of magic, one must first diagnose and analyze one's natal relationship to the stars and the gemstones to which they correspond. The correspondences of the Navaratna are:

- Ruby—the Sun
- Pearl—the Moon
- Red coral—Mars
- Emerald—Mercury
- Yellow sapphire—Jupiter
- Diamond—Venus
- Blue sapphire—Saturn
- Hessonite garnet—Rahu (North Node)
- Cat's eye—Ketu (South Node)

In Vedic or Hindu astrology, life on Earth is said to be influenced primarily by the *Navagraha* or nine planets; the *Navaratna*, or nine lucky gems, represent the Navagraha. When used together, they can protect the bearer from harm and disease by balancing potentially negative effects of the planets they represent. The specific configuration of the Navaratna is a map of the nine planets in the cosmos as well as a map of the entire cosmos. The Navaratna must be worn with ruby, which represents the Sun, pointing due north. Then, ruby must be followed, clockwise from the top, by diamond, pearl, coral, hessonite garnet, blue sapphire, cat's eye chrysoberyl, yellow sapphire, and emerald. It is inauspicious to substitute other crystals. Some Vedic astrologers caution that not all nine stones are recommended or tolerable for anyone at any given time, and misaligned combinations of stones may activate unwanted portions of the energy field, overwhelming the human system and disrupting important balances. This chapter features the stones of the Navaratna not mentioned elsewhere in this book and other crystals from India.

> In Vedic or Hindu astrology, life on Earth is said to be influenced primarily by the *Navagraha* or nine planets; the *Navaratna*, or nine lucky gems, represent the Navagraha.

CRYSTALS OF INDIA AT A GLANCE

CRYSTAL	PROPERTIES	PLACE OF ORIGIN (Ancient and Modern)
Cat's eye chrysoberyl	In the Navaratna, represents Ketu, intuition, and sensitivity.	Brazil, India, China, Africa, Sri Lanka, United States
Diamond	clarity, strength, endurance, power, focus, will, commitment In the Navaratna, represents Venus and feminine beauty.	Egypt, Columbia
Lepidocrocite	relief from anxiety, depression, restless energy	India, Brazil, Spain
Red coral	fertility, power In the Navaratna, represents physical strength and courage in battle.	India, Japan, Mediterranean Sea
Ruby	In the Navaratna, represents the Sun and passion as well as personal power.	India, Sri Lanka, Burma
Sapphire	In the Navaratna, blue sapphire represents Saturn (physical health and well-being) and yellow sapphire represents Jupiter (wisdom, compassion).	India, Sri Lanka, Burma
Shiva lingam	balance of divine feminine and masculine, sex, sensuality, passion, and intimacy	India
Zeolites	upper chakra opening, accessing Akashic records, spiritual awakening, quantum healing	India

CAT`S EYE CHRYSOBERYL

Popular in ancient times, but lesser known today, chrysoberyl derives its name from the Greek word *chrysos,* or "golden," and *beryllos,* for its beryllium content (and from which the modern gemstone name *beryl* derives). Used for protection among ancient Roman soldiers who believed it was uniquely protective in battle, it is thought today to bring personal power and self-confidence to the bearer.

In the Navaratna, chrysoberyl represents Ketu or the South Node, and, if well positioned, brings harmony, intuition, peace, and the unveiling of spiritual gifts. In Asia and the Middle East, chrysoberyl is recommended to protect against the evil eye. In modern metaphysical traditions, chrysoberyl is prized as a rare gem of the solar plexus chakra. By holding chrysoberyl, it is said one is naturally guided toward the best outcome when an important decision must be made. In Western evolutionary astrology, the South Node indicates karmic work from your past lifetime. It makes sense this power crystal holds the wisdom of what came before, and your soul's evolution since your last lifetime, to guide you toward self-actualization. A well-placed South Node is said to ensure long life, and modern legends of this crystal also speak of energies of immortality, rejuvenation, and transformation. Perhaps the most magical thing about this particular crystal, however, is its growth structure; raw chrysoberyl crystals exhibit a perfect six-pointed star resembling the rays of the Sun high in the sky on a summer day.

DIAMOND

Of all the precious gemstones on the planet, diamond has the longest lineage of magic and legend. In ancient times, diamonds were used for protection and to guard against enemies. In fact, at one time in ancient Rome, diamonds were believed to be poisonous and were fed to enemies to safeguard kings, queens, and warriors. The most precious of the nine Navaratna stones, diamonds were a sacred reward to victorious soldiers in battle. In the Navaratna, diamonds represent feminine beauty and the planet Venus, or Shukra, offering qualities of beauty, grace, and charisma to the bearer.

Today most diamonds are mined in Africa and Israel, but India was once the queen of diamond production. In fact, diamonds were not mined outside India until the nineteenth century, and, until the discovery of diamonds in Brazil in the eighteenth century, India was the *only* source of diamonds.

Diamond is associated with Venus in Vedic astrology, which is considered a helpful planet, so most people can safely wear diamonds without negative energetic consequences. Indian mythology advises wearing only high quality diamonds, if possible, to attract the best outcomes and energies; in general, Indians believed the higher the quality of a stone, the more powerful its healing and magical properties.

One of the largest diamonds in the world, the Koh-i-Noor (Arabic for "mountain of light"), resides in the Tower of London, where millions of visitors view it each year. The estimated weight of the Koh-i-Noor diamond is 105.6 carats, and it was last worn by Queen Elizabeth, the Queen Mother. The Indian government has claimed ownership of the diamond since 1947, when India gained independence from the United Kingdom.

The process of locating diamond deposits is made easier by a mineral named kimberlite, a carrier of diamonds; when a miner locates kimberlite, it is assured diamonds are nearby. Kimberlite is named for Kimberley, South Africa, where a major diamond mine was located in the nineteenth century.

Diamond's rarity explains part of our universal and eternal fascination with this carbon-based mineral. Today the phrase "blood diamond" is part of our common vernacular and refers to conflict diamonds mined in dangerous war zones. But throughout history, diamonds have accumulated a vast lineage of mystical tales, capturing the human imagination and perpetuating their perceived value in the marketplace. Long ago, Jewish priests believed that, when placed before an innocent person, an authentic diamond would glow brightly and clearly, but when placed before a guilty person, would grow dark and opaque. Diamonds

were believed to cure hundreds of ailments, including infections, cardiac problems, depression, and anxiety. Ancient Romans thought diamonds were the tears of the gods, and Roman mythology describes Cupid's arrows as tipped with diamonds. Greek philosopher Plato referred to diamonds as falling stars, ancient remnants of the birth of the star constellations. Today's brides overwhelmingly prefer a flawless round diamond for their engagement rings, a symbol of power, fidelity, and enduring affection. Ancient Greek physician Dioscorides, author of *De Materia Medica*, referred to diamond, between 50 and 70 CE, as a, "precious stone of reconciliation and love"; almost two thousand years later, in 1947, DeBeers declared, "a diamond is forever"—one of the most famous advertising slogans in history.

Diamond is produced under extreme pressure within the ground; once formed, diamonds emerge toward Earth's surface to cool. Modern metaphysical correspondences for diamond reflect the growth process of this mineral; it is said to strengthen the bearer, helping him or her endure difficult circumstances or hardships in service of spiritual development or advancement. Diamonds grow in a natural octahedral shape—a shape that activates energetic frequencies known as "diamond codes." These codes are embedded within the energetic fields of all humans and can be accessed and activated by working with crystals that grow in the octahedral structure (also octahedral by nature is fluorite, the stone of *dharma*, or soul purpose).

Perhaps the universal application of diamonds as the preferred choice for wedding adornment reflects not only the rarity of this mineral but the extensive history it carries as a crystal of strength, tenacity, endurance, and commitment. Diamond is the only mineral to score a full 10/10 on the Measure of Hardness Scale (MOHS), meaning, while nothing can cut it, it can be used to cut other materials. Diamonds can be used to reinforce your personal strength and energetic reserves during periods of adrenal fatigue or psychic stress.

HESSONITE GARNET

In Vedic astrology, hessonite garnet or *gomed* is associated with Rahu, the northern, or ascending, lunar node in Western astrology. The name *hessonite* derives from the Greek *hesson*, or "inferior," referring to the evil nature of the Vedic planet Rahu, which is associated with negative influences.

To transmute Rahu energy, especially among those with a northern node in Capricorn, wear hessonite on the middle finger, which is associated with Saturn, Capricorn's ruling planet. A hessonite of exceptionally fine quality, no fewer than two carats, should be chosen. Wearing hessonite helps balance the overtly masculine energies of fear, agitation, anger, and confusion, bringing clarity, balance, and calmness to the mind. In addition, hessonite is rumored to reverse all forms of dark magic and transmute dark energetic code, keeping the wearer safe from physical and energetic harm. Worn in the correct size and form, hessonite garnet is said to bestow great wealth and material prosperity upon its wearer, especially when set in silver, gold, copper, or a variation of those metals. Ideally, a gomed (hessonite) ring is worn first on a Saturday, the day of the week associated with its ruling planet, Saturn. Hessonite garnet heals and aligns the lower chakras, instantly bestowing a sense of deep peace and spiritual protection.

LEPIDOCROCITE

Lepidocrocite is an enchanting stone; it contains a world within of sparkling red slivers of light that dazzle the eye and spark the imagination. The name *lepidocrocite* comes from the Greek words *lipis*, or "scale," and *krokis*, or "fiber"——a quite literal description of the inclusions within.

The red inclusions inside lepidocrocite are hematite, which brings balance and grounding——but in micronized form, which is much easier for the subtle body to integrate than larger pieces. Thus, for empaths who seek protection and clearing, lepidocrocite is a better choice than hematite, which can overwhelm the empath's delicate systems.

Lepidocrocite often grows with quartz, amethyst, and goethite, and it is part of the Super Seven configuration of master healing minerals. Lepidocrocite is a relatively new mineral to the crystal world, so legends of its powers are still developing. In metaphysical circles, it is said to heal the heart and lungs, because it purifies and detoxifies the physical and auric bodies of external toxins while raising internal frequencies. This simultaneous release-and-receive movement of energy facilitates transmutation, even allowing the release of stored memories thousands of years old while attracting new frequencies to replace what is voided. All this happens spontaneously and as needed when working with lepidocrocite; for that reason, it is known as a powerful talisman for anyone with post-traumatic stress disorder.

RED CORAL

Red coral is like the life force, mana, or prana, of made matter; holding it, working with it, you feel connected to the umbilical cord of the entire planet. In Vedic astrology, it represents Mars, the planet of strength, vitality, and sexuality. Red coral is the lifeblood of the underwater kingdom and holds the wisdom of all water spirits. Legends of its use in fertility rites abound across many cultures. The Navajo combined red coral with turquoise for fertility; in Native American cosmology, red coral represents the veins in the right, or feminine, side of the body, while turquoise represents the veins in the left, or masculine, side. Wearing both together acknowledges their sacred union. Red coral's connection to fertility is based primarily and historically on its bright red color and its resemblance to freshly drawn or menstrual blood. In Scotland, red coral amulets were traditionally worn for protection of the life force. Beyond its association with the life force, red coral offers strength and energy to the wearer. In Vedic astrology, red coral is contraindicated for anyone with anger issues or an inability to manage their emotions, as it can cause a tendency toward hostility and inclination toward excessive force. This energy can be useful for some but highly destructive for others. Red coral has also been considered a cause of high fever and should not be used by those with active infections or illness.

RUBY

Ruby is the queen of the gemstone world and the birthstone of all July babies. Where her true legends begin, almost no one knows. Today crystal healers rely on ruby for passion and use it to heal heartache. But in ancient times, rubies were believed to grant instant protection. In fact, Egyptian pharaohs believed ruby granted immediate and eternal protection, prosperity, and peace to the bearer. Ancient jewelers began to set a single ruby on the *inside* of rings to help one travel safely through life; mothers wore bands with inset rubies to protect their babies during pregnancy. Ancient Indians also believed rubies reunited lovers and helped lovers hold memories of their beloved in their heart during periods of separation.

Modern metaphysical legends teach that rubies are the spirits of our deceased ancestors and when we lose a loved one in this lifetime they go on to live forever as rubies in our hearts. In Reiki practice, rubies represent the life force and are used in crystal healing to represent and enhance flow of the wearer's prana or chi. Red is the color of the reincarnation of Buddha, and Hindus consider red the most sacred color of the gods. It is no surprise, then, that Shah Jahan placed a wreath of ruby roses on the tomb of his wife, Mumtaz Majal, at the Taj Majal, the temple he built to honor their lives while she was alive.[5]

He must have known that, in ancient India, rubies were considered *ratnaraj*, or the king of gems, and ancient Hindu tradition held that those who made the offering of a ruby to Krishna would be granted eternal life as emperors (if the stone was small, the giver would be reborn a king).[6] Even today monarchs of every major country are drawn to ruby, though several of the modern English monarchy's rubies were later tested and discovered to be spinel. Until the twentieth century, almost the entire world's supply of rubies came exclusively from Burma, which meant other red stones often confused with ruby were likely crystals with a similar physical appearance; to the eye, ruby and spinel are often surprisingly similar in clarity and color. Large rubies, over 20 carats, were considered the exclusive property of Burmese kings, so it is rare to find any rubies of that size today. Those that remain from Burma have, in many cases, been cut and sold as smaller gemstones to maximize profit.

In the Navaratna, ruby represents the Sun, or Surya. As the solar crystal of the nine Navaratna stones, ruby is thought to bring strength, self-reliance, and leadership as well as passion, purpose, and positional power. Ruby is best worn as the center stone of a ring on the ring finger of the right hand; in the Navaratna, ruby is always set in the center to represent the strength of the Sun's dominant position in the sky.

SAPPHIRE

Sapphire and ruby are both members of the corundum family, precious gemstones with a hardness score of 9 on the Measure of Hardness Scale (MOHS). When corundum is red, it's ruby; when corundum is blue or yellow, it's sapphire.

BLUE SAPPHIRE

Blue sapphire is the most common member of the sapphire family, though sapphire grows naturally in a wide range of colors. Blue sapphire has long been considered a crystal for psychic development and wisdom; in fact, it is often referred to as the teacher's stone, especially helpful for articulating and translating complex ideas. In the Navaratna, blue sapphire represents Saturn, or Shani. In astrology, Saturn is a karmic planet that defines major periods in an individual's life and governs life lessons as well as life cycles. When used correctly, according to Vedic astrology, blue sapphire can bring great wealth, clarity, and even prestige. Depending on the placement of Saturn in the natal chart, one may or may not be recommended to work with blue sapphire. If recommended based on Saturn placement, it is best to wear sapphires of perfect quality set in gold on the middle finger.

Outside India, blue sapphire may well be one of the most easily confused gemstones in history. Our ancient ancestors referred to many different "blue stones" as sapphire, including lapis lazuli (see page 46). Understanding and identifying differences in crystalline structure would have helped our ancestors accurately identify one from the other; sapphire grows along a hexagonal crystal structure, while lapis lazuli has a very different internal cubic structure. Today we are far less likely to confuse any crystal for another. But long ago, such mistakes were common and, thus, we read between the lines of crystal legends to accurately discern which crystals are being referred to, when, and for what purpose.

Today most blue sapphires come from India, where sapphires continue to be mined in relatively good supply. The finest quality sapphires in the world have always come from Ceylon, known today as Sri Lanka. Even today Ceylon sapphires are considered the most beautiful on Earth, and Sri Lankan sapphires are also the largest ever mined. The world's three largest sapphires—the Blue Giant of the Orient at 466 carats, the Logan Blue at 423 carats, and the Blue Bell of Asia at 400 carats—were all mined in Sri Lanka. Large blue star sapphires, also primarily from Sri Lanka and so called because they display a perfect six-pointed star across the stone's top when cut *en cabochon* (shaped and polished as opposed to faceted), are the rarest of all sapphires. Star sapphires (and rubies) represent less than 5 percent of all sapphires and are said to harness the energy of all the sacred elements and geometries within their form. Modern magical practitioners seek star sapphires for their wisdom, magic, and mystical powers steeped in history and mystery. Recently, a pocket of rare sapphires with trigons on their faces emerged in India and have been a source of fascination within the metaphysical community, as until they emerged no one had seen trigons on sapphire before. Even today new crystal legends are being written as new stones and new forms of familiar stones emerge from Gaia's womb.

YELLOW SAPPHIRE

Because it represents Jupiter (and the god Brihaspati) in the Navaratna, yellow sapphire shares the energy streams of wisdom and expanded consciousness with its blue sapphire sibling. Brihaspati is said to be the teacher of all Hindu gods, and so it holds the wisdom energy stream while also activating one's center of personal power. Because yellow sapphire activates a different chakra than blue sapphire—the solar plexus for will and personal power versus the third eye for intuition and inner knowing—yellow sapphire enhances joy, personal power, and optimism. When well aspected in the Vedic astrological profile, it supports happiness, prosperity, and wealth. However, if Jupiter is weak within one's chart, yellow sapphire can attract the opposite, ushering in feelings of unworthiness and depression. In general, yellow sapphire facilitates self-actualization and self-realization, the union of the self with God consciousness.

Like the finest blue sapphires, high quality yellow sapphires also come from Sri Lanka. To harness the fortune-bearing properties of Jupiter, it is best to set yellow sapphire in gold and wear on the ring finger of one's writing hand. In Western cosmology, yellow sapphire is said to bring deep rest, comfort, and even sleep to the bearer. By calming the nervous mind and inviting meditative energies to emerge, yellow sapphire inspires a sense that all is well in the universe.

SHIVA LINGAM

In Sanskrit, *shiva lingam* (sometimes referred to as *shivling*) translates to "mark" or innate quality of Shiva, the god of all creation. Although many have suggested shiva lingam is a reference to the male phallus, this elongated egg-shaped sacred talisman is much more than that; Shiva is the ultimate unity of the divine feminine and masculine, and cannot be reduced to a single sexual organ or energetic stream, though physical displays of passion and desire are some of Shiva's gifts.

Found along the Narmada River in western India, known as the river of blessings, shiva lingam is a sacred form of micro-cryptocrystalline quartz said to have shattered and coagulated within Earth following a massive meteoric collision thousands of years ago. The Narmada River is also known as the mother river; the word *narmada* literally means sweet ("nar"), and mother ("mata" or "mada"). Whatever comes from her sacred waters is also sacred and brings with it blessings of prosperity, passion, and peace. Shiva lingam is a blessing of creation brought forward along the rivers of the Great Mother. It is the divine union of sacred feminine and masculine energies, united at last in one place, honoring the sanctity of life.

These incredible crystals date back to the Vedas (around 1500 BCE), and their legacy endures today as a testament to the universal need and desire for balance in all things. So important was their presence, and so holy their origin, ancient Romans adopted the shape and form in their *Prayapas*, which were used in the Roman empire as tools to worship Shiva and pray for blessings once the practice and tradition spread west. Shiva lingam are even referred to in Hollywood: The Sankara Stone in *Indiana Jones and the Temple of Doom* is, in fact, a shiva lingam.

Shiva lingam appear naturally along the Narmada River in two colors: variegated red/brown and pure black, said to be meteoric in nature. In the traditional variegated shiva lingam, red and brown markings represent blood and feminine energy while tan, neutral background colors represent masculine energy. A well-balanced piece with even markings in both shades is considered of the highest quality and purity. The lines are also said to reflect the markings on Shiva's forehead. When shiva lingam wash up along the Narmada's banks, where they are gathered once a year at the beginning of monsoon season when water levels are lowest, each is hand-polished and readied for the marketplace. Black shiva lingam are far rarer, and, legend says, when a black shiva washed upon the shores in India in ancient times, a temple was immediately erected in the exact location of its sighting. If black shiva are meteoric and, thus, contain particles of extraterrestrial matter, this explains the value and legends assigned to this rare crystal. Smaller black shivas are relatively accessible today but larger pieces are considered collector's items of enormous value.

ZEOLITE

One thinks of zeolite as a relative newcomer to the crystal and mineral world because it was only widely recognized and named in the eighteenth century by the Swedish mineralogist Cronstedt who formally identified it. The name *zeolite* is an amalgam of the Greek words *zeo*, meaning "boil" and *lithose*, meaning "stone," because when you boil zeolites they release water in the form of steam. Zeolites have been used by NASA to grow plants in space, and by skincare companies because of its absorbent ability to transfer moisture. These varied utilities are just some reasons zeolite is known as the "miracle mineral."

Zeolites have been used historically in water filtration systems and are known in the metaphysical community to purify and detoxify the human energetic field.

The most well-known and popular metaphysical member of the zeolite family, apophyllite, is discussed in detail on the following page.

APOPHYLLITE

The mystical queen of the zeolite family is no doubt apophyllite, with its glimmering prisms of light shining from across a room. Apophyllite's points are like gleaming pyramids of radiant energy, and while it occurs naturally in many colors from white or clear to green, yellow, pink, red, and even a rare light brown, clear apophyllite is the most common and easily recognizable. Apophyllite has a high water content and is considered a heart chakra as well as a soul star chakra gemstone that provides emotional healing and purification through ascension and connection to source energy. The pyramid-shaped crystals of apophyllite are said to be doorways to other dimensions, through which one can easily access the Akashic records or galactic library. By looking through the bottom of an apophyllite termination toward the apex, one opens an interdimensional light portal or stargate. This stargate can be entered in meditation to access deeper levels of conscious and psychic development, as well as for astral travel and dream-state journeywork. Though anyone can work with any crystal at any time if called, most crystal healers consider apophyllite a more advanced stone, one especially well-suited for Reiki healing because of its ability to clearly channel universal light energy.

ACCESSING CRYSTAL WISDOM: INDIA

If you wish to receive the wisdom of India and connect to her majesty via her crystals, choose two crystals that come from her sacred land and hold one in each hand. Bring both hands to prayer pose over your heart, and bring your full attention to your breath. Imagine India's sacred rivers running through your veins; incense smoke rising from her temples becomes your breath. Allow all parts of you to align with the cardinal elements and from there, slip even more deeply into the primal rhythms of your soul as it merges with hers. From this place of divine alignment, all miracles are possible. Where will you direct this powerful energy stream and to what end(s)?

APOPHYLLITE

Apophyllite **opens ascension gateways** and **deepens meditative states** to help you access new levels of awareness. Being drawn to apophyllite can be a sign to attend to your spiritual development. Access the Akashic records in meditation for wisdom to guide this process.

CAT'S EYE CHRYSOBERYL

Chrysoberyl is a divine keeper of **wisdom of the past and present**, illuminating **karmic connections and synchronicities** to empower and inspire you. When you feel incapable or need a boost of creative inspiration or self-confidence, let chrysoberyl activate your power center for a sense of possibility, competence, and encouragement. By protecting you and shielding you from unwanted influences, chrysoberyl helps you avoid distractions and fear to stay focused on your path.

DIAMOND

Diamond holds energies of **resilience** and **strength**, promising the bearer good health and good fortune. Work with diamond in meditation to **discern your personal light codes**, or unique energetic signature, that you transfer to others during healing work. Diamond can also help you understand your soul path, especially when used with fluorite.

HESSONITE GARNET

A stone of abundance, hessonite garnet helps you **attract long-term wealth** and align yourself with **energetic frequencies of success**. Hessonite garnet helps manifest money by revealing new sources of financial opportunity. It also activates the lower chakras and protects your energetic field from unwanted influences.

LEPIDOCROCITE

An emotional healer, lepidocrocite **helps unravel karmic tensions** and **relieves energetic stress**. It is helpful for anyone suffering from post-traumatic stress disorder, as it helps identify and release the root cause of old trauma in stored memory. Lepidocrocite automatically replaces low vibrations with higher frequencies, which explains its reputation as a master healer and purifier of energy.

RED CORAL

Red coral **enhances the life force** and **promotes fertility** of new life, new ideas, and new projects. Its vital energetic field nourishes the prana or chi and dissolves blockages preventing strong energetic flow within the body. Red coral also energizes the central nervous system and the lower chakras, helping one feel calm, safe, and grounded.

RUBY

Ruby is the life force in crystal form and is recommended for healing both **emotional** and **physical issues** of the heart. Ruby helps one find one's passion and recommit to goals with enthusiasm and confidence. Ruby also attracts love to the bearer and can help you overcome fear and heartache from past trauma.

BLUE SAPPHIRE

Blue sapphire is for wisdom and is considered the **most powerful talisman for teachers** and sages. It activates the third eye chakra, connecting your intellectual mind with your intuition. In this way, blue sapphire is a channeling stone that helps you receive and accurately transmit universal wisdom to your audience.

YELLOW SAPPHIRE

Yellow sapphire brings **joy** and **optimism**. It also attracts good fortune and good luck—especially in business and intellectual matters. Yellow sapphire calms a nervous mind and can help you focus on details and tasks if you are easily distracted.

SHIVA LINGAM

Shiva lingam represents the **balance of the divine feminine and divine masculine**, helping you integrate masculine and feminine energies in your life for wellness, peace, and alignment. Shiva lingam also represents sexual desire and lust, as well as the physical consummation of spiritual commitment. Place in your sacred space to remind you of the sacred union of the spiritual and the material present in all forms of life.

Chapter 4

CRYSTALS OF MINOA, GREECE, AND ROME

Most timelines place the start of the Greek Empire around 1200 BCE and the beginning of the Roman Empire around 800 BCE. They're considered the birthplaces of Western civilization and culture. At this time, ancient Egypt was experiencing radical shifts in leadership, and such instability created rich opportunities for the establishment of stable leadership and order elsewhere in the world.

U ltimately, the Greeks were conquered by the Romans in 146 BCE, but a modern era was taking shape. Fresh perspectives and technological advancements substantially improved the quality of human life and health. One such advancement was the development of Roman aqueduct systems in 300 BCE, allowing for safe transport of fresh water to different parts of Rome, which facilitated the rise of modern communities and allowed for the creation of water features such as public bathhouses and ornamental fountains. In ancient Rome, if you had water, you had money. Roman aqueducts were lined with shungite, a carbon-based mineral that naturally detoxifies and purifies water, removing most harmful bacteria. In fact, it is said certain rivers in Russia produce perfect drinking water because it has been consistently exposed to shungite over thousands of years.

Most uses of crystals in ancient Greece and Rome, however, were ornamental and aesthetic. Gemstones and crystal carvings were made into amulets and jewelry. Signet rings—statement rings with a gemstone stamp bearing the signature of a person, family, or dynasty—originated in Greece and spread west to Rome. Men traditionally wore one ring with their signet on the right hand, or the king's hand, and used it as a seal upon hot wax to sign official documents. Owning a signet ring was a sign of wealth and aristocracy. Every aspect of the creation of signet rings was intentional and meticulous—from the choice of material to the design, the process, and finally the setting. Most signet rings were carved *intaglio*, derived from the Latin word for "to cut into." Intaglio pieces in Rome were often carved from agate, including carnelian and sardonyx imported from India. Today many of these original pieces reside in the world's most famous museums, including the J. Paul Getty Museum in Malibu, California, and the British Museum in London.

Greeks and Romans had access to more crystals and gemstones than you might imagine via established trade routes along the Silk Road. Alexander the Great is largely responsible for Greek and Roman exposure to Asia. He conquered Persian forces and then brought arms to southern India. As a result, Greeks and Romans were able to purchase precious gems from India, including rubies, emeralds, and sapphires, as well as many semi-precious crystals from the Middle East and Egypt. This allowed them to explore crystals' softness for carving and their energies for ritual and ceremonial purposes.

This experimentation yielded the first expansive wisdom about the mystical properties of crystals. Could a crystal ward off intoxication? Could a crystal protect you from evil spirits or prevent your enemies from seeing you in battle? The Greeks and Romans were intent on answering such questions, and their empires are fertile grounds for rich exploration of the legends surrounding crystals today. They used wine and other intoxicants to quiet their conscious minds to hear the voices of the gods, which guided not only the way they lived their lives and governed their cities but shaped their perspectives on life, death, and the afterlife.

CRYSTALS OF GREECE AND ROME AT A GLANCE

CRYSTAL	PROPERTIES	PLACE OF ORIGIN (Ancient and Modern)
Amber	physical protection, physical healing, exorcism, psychic protection	Baltic Sea, Middle and Far East
Amethyst	peace, balance, detoxification	Greece, Brazil
Carnelian/ Sard	energy, power, enthusiasm	India
Opal	transformation, will of the gods	Australia, Africa
Pearl	emotional healing and balance	Southeast Asia, Persian Gulf
Quartz	magnification, intensification of energy, expansion, power	all countries/all continents
Selenite	harnessing Moon's magic and energy, divine feminine power and beauty, magnification of wealth and influence	Spain and traded throughout Middle and Far East
Topaz	protection from enemies, invisibility, discernment in battle	Brazil, India, Australia, Mexico, Africa

AMBER

Amber was important to ancient Romans, and fascinating tales of its origin and mythological magic endure today. Ancient Romans used it as a pliable and powerful carving material for sacred amulets, connecting them to the spirit world. From the Latin word *ambrum* comes the Arabic *anbar*, which is the ancient root of our modern English word *amber*.

Amber, or the fossilized resin of trees, was sourced in the northern Baltic regions during the Roman Republic era and imported south because of its growing reputation as a crystal of power and protection, including its perceived ability to ward off evil and cure mysterious diseases. Although European and Sicilian sources of amber existed at the time, Baltic Sea amber was considered then—as today—a superior source in terms of energy, wisdom, and vibration. In the Baltic, this Earth-based mineral meets water to take on new and unique energetic properties. It can ground you and awaken you to ancient memories of your wisdom, truth, and purpose. It can heal a millennia of soul traumas if you work with it or wear it for extended periods.

In Rome, myths were considered important sources of wisdom, truths that stood the test of time. Ovid, author of *Metamorphoses*, spoke of amber as the crystalline tears of Clymene and her daughters, who were transformed into poplar trees after the death of Phaethon, Clymene's son, who tried to drive his father Helios's chariot across the sky. Indeed, the concept of amber resin as tears of sacred beings endures through more modern Renaissance literary traditions; Othello describes human pain as similar to a weeping tree, where tears drop "of one whose subdued eyes / Albeit unused to the melting mood / Drops tears as fast as the Arabian trees / Their medicinable gum."[7] This medicinal gum held sacred wisdom for Romans and Greeks, who began to carve and polish jewelry and amulets from the mystical resin. If amber is the basis of our tears, and the proper medicine of grief, then perhaps the material itself has cleansing properties worthy of exploration. And although the conifer forests that produced Baltic amber became extinct rough forty million years ago, the energy of this material lives on in the stories and myths that have survived far beyond its formation.

Two kinds of amber, though virtually incomparable to us today, were prized in ancient times: yellow amber, a form of tree resin, and gray amber, or *ambergris*, a solid but waxy material formed as a byproduct of the sperm whale's digestive system. Ambergris became a popular ingredient in perfume and resins, though it is illegal to harvest today because of the whales' endangered state. Synthetic alternatives and formulations of resin combinations have come close to replicating the scent of ambergris, though nothing is exactly the same, either in scent or metaphysical properties.

Pliny the Elder disputed the Greek and Roman origin stories of amber, noting descendants of Germania referred to amber as *glaesum*, a substance derived from pine trees, which was discernable upon burning by its distinctive pine odor. Pliny also suggested the drops of resin were formed by the sea rather than over the course of millions of years through fossilization—an allusion perhaps to ambergris and amber resin and an attempt to reconcile their diverse points of origin.

Greeks and Romans believed amber held mystical properties that kept the wearer safe from harm, attracted to them what they sought, and even made them insusceptible to disease. Inside Roman cemeteries to this day, one can find child burial sites adorned with amber beads designed as protective amulets to help carry the child's spirit to safe eternal rest. Perhaps the fact that amber contains succinic acid, a powerful natural antibiotic, gave rise to rumors of its medicinal and protective properties. Pliny cites the Latin name *succinum*, alluding to this key ingredient in raw amber material. Ancient Persians believed rubbing amber attracted light objects, including grass and wheat, to it, so they named it *kahruba* or "straw robber."

For these reasons and more, amber maintains a mysterious reputation even among modern metaphysical audiences. Because it was largely reserved for those with vast economic resources, including those with royal authority and divine right power, amber will likely continue to be a collectible resource for centuries to come. In modern metaphysical circles it is used for psychic protection and healing.

AMETHYST

Today amethyst is considered a crystal for balance, peace, and detoxification; these modern metaphysical properties have their roots in ancient language and tradition. In Greek, *amethystos* means "not drunk."

In ancient Rome, wine festivals honoring Dionysus, the Roman god of agriculture and the wine harvest, were a regular tradition. At these intoxicating festivals, wine was said to reveal truth and wisdom by blocking the conscious mind and lowering inhibitions. In Greece, Bacchus was revered as the god of pleasure and wine, and his festivals involved wild and indulgent explorations through wine and deep intoxication that led to mystical revelations. As legend goes, Bacchus fell in love with Amethyst, a beautiful maiden, but she spurned his advances. He vowed to seek revenge on her. Artemis took pity on the maiden and turned her into a crystalline quartz statue to protect her. Bacchus became enraged and saddened, pouring his chalice of wine over the statue, turning it light purple. From that myth and the word's etymology come both the ancient and modern uses of amethyst—to prevent drunkenness and loss of control.

To ancient Greeks and Romans, drunkenness was a sign of weakness. To the Greeks in particular, loss of control meant one was vulnerable to enemy attack. However, Greeks loved to drink wine. Romans adored wine, too; in fact, we get the famous saying *in vino veritas*, "in wine truth," from ancient Rome. Greeks and Romans drank wine from amethyst goblets on ceremonial occasions to help wine reveal its truth without also revealing the bearer's weakness.

CARNELIAN | SARD

Carnelian is a member of the chalcedony family, a microcrystalline type of quartz; its name derives from the Latin word *cornum*, meaning cherry. In ancient Greece and Rome, carnelian of a dark red-brown color was referred to as *sard*, which comes from the Persian word for red-yellow color, *sered*. Pliny the Elder claimed the name *sard* comes from the name of a Lydian city, Sardis. Sardis was captured by Cyrus the Great of Persia and remained a Persian territory until Alexander the Great defeated Cyrus in 334 BCE.

Many of the prized signet rings of Rome were carved from carnelian. It was relatively easy to carve, and wax does not adhere easily to agate or chalcedony. Carnelian's naturally variegated shades of gold, orange, and red also created striking sculptures. In the second century BCE, Damigeron claimed sard made a woman "lovable" if she wore it.[8] Carnelian's second written mention, in 300 BCE, comes from Theophrastus, who referred to a red stone called *odem* with similar colors and markings. Interestingly, odem is the first stone listed of those gemstones in the breastplate of the Bible, in the book of Exodus. The red-orange-yellow coloration of carnelian is associated with power, since early Egypt and the rise of Ra, whose legends were well known in Rome. Thus, a gold, orange, or red stone would have been associated with potency, virility, and physical strength as well as wealth, power, and authority.

OPAL

The most famous piece of jewelry in Roman lore was not a signet ring; rather, it was a massive rare opal ring Marc Antony was rumored to have sourced for his beloved Cleopatra. Mark Antony was very fond of gemstones and often gave them to Cleopatra as gifts. On one such famous occasion, he tried to purchase a large and beautiful opal from Roman general Marcus Nonius, offering a vast fortune for it. However, such was the opal's beauty, Nonius refused and was given an ultimatum by the furious Mark Antony: Either sell the ring or leave town. Nonius chose to leave Rome and keep the opal.

Opal's name comes from the Sanskrit *upala*, meaning "precious stone," and Latin *opalus*, meaning "change color." Greeks believed opals were formed wherever the gods stepped foot on Earth. In fact, one Greek myth suggests Mount Olympus is made entirely of opals, from the footsteps of Zeus and the entire pantheon of Greek gods and goddesses. Greek poet Onomakritos wrote of opals in his sixth-century poem, paying homage to their inner fire. Roman opals came from Slovakia, known now as Hungarian opals, and would have been very costly. The Nonius ring, which contained a hazelnut-size carved opal gem, was valued at 2,000,000 sesterces, the equivalent of $200,000 to $300,000 in today's (U.S.) currency.

PEARL

In Rome, pearls were referred to as *unio*, or "unique," because Romans recognized no two pearls were alike. They have enjoyed a lengthy and well-earned reputation for having magical powers. Before the advent of cultured pearls, natural pearls were so elusive and costly only the wealthiest and most powerful people owned them. At the height of the Roman Empire, one general allegedly financed an entire war by selling a single large pearl taken from his mother's earrings.

What drove this near obsession with this watery treasure? In ancient Rome, pearls came from only two sources: the Persian Gulf and Southeast Asia. Both places were rumored sources of luck, power, and wisdom. The journey to acquire a pearl was costly and difficult. As a result, Greeks or Romans possessing pearls signified great wealth. Romans of high station sewed pearls onto their furniture and into their clothing to bring luck and prosperity. Cleopatra once wagered Marc Antony that she could host the most lavish dinner in history. As Pliny the Elder recounts, Mark Antony sat back in his seat watching in awe as Cleopatra took off one of her large pearl earrings, broke off the pearl, dropped it in her glass, and drank the wine—pearl included. The value of the pearl she swallowed is estimated at 60 million sesterces, or roughly $6 million today.

QUARTZ

Quartz is a common mineral; by its mineralogical name, silicon dioxide, it is found on every continent throughout the world. And it has a very strong energetic vibration or resonance. Quartz can raise a person's personal vibration or enhance a cosmic vibration to raise energy for the entire planet—the entire cosmos, even.

The first reference to the word *quartz* dates to 1530, when it was described by Georgius Agricola, a German metallurgist who pioneered the field of mineralogy and modern geology. Over time, quartz was referred to as rock quartz and then rock crystal, which is where our modern perception of quartz originates. The Greek word for crystal is *krystallos*, meaning "ice." Ancient Greeks believed quartz was god-created ice so powerful it could not melt. Greeks and Romans were among the first to identify quartz as a powerful crystal and begin to carve amulets from it.

Quartz is not only diverse in its growth patterns, it is diverse in appearance, too. Rose quartz is pink; smoky quartz is brown; citrine is yellow; and amethyst is purple. They share the same basic mineral structure and chemical composition, though their metaphysical meanings are as diverse and beautiful as their colors.

ROSE QUARTZ

Romans believed rose quartz prevented early aging and brought romantic love; stories with origins in Egypt say Cleopatra placed pieces of this lovely pink stone in her milk-based facial and bath elixirs. In Greece and Rome, rose quartz was seen as a gift from Cupid and Eros—Roman and Greek gods of romantic love, respectively. Today rose quartz is commonly used in spells and enchantments to attract romantic and spiritual love. Another Greek myth weaves a tale of Adonis and Aphrodite, lovers and twin spirits separated by death. Adonis, Greek god of rebirth and reincarnation, was the beloved of Aphrodite, who raised him from birth. One day while Aphrodite was away, Adonis ventured into the forest to hunt. He was warned to avoid anyone who denied his divinity. Ares, Aphrodite's former lover, had grown jealous of Aphrodite's passion and love for Adonis, and disguised himself as a wild boar. Ares attacked Adonis, nearly killing him. By the time Aphrodite found him, Adonis was inhaling his last breath. Aphrodite, in her grief, wept for Adonis and screamed cries of sadness to the gods on Mount Olympus. She sprinkled him with her tears, which were said to be the nectar of the gods, and sang to him sacred songs of survival and love. However, she arrived too late and Adonis had already crossed to the land of the dead. Where Adonis's blood touched the ground, anemones grew—the deep red flowers represented immortal love. Where Aphrodite's tears touched the ground mixing with Adonis's blood, rose quartz was born in honor of their eternal union.

SELENITE

Greeks and Romans found innovative ways to incorporate crystals when building important structures. Ancient Greeks believed the Greek goddess of the Moon, Selene, was trapped inside gypsum-based selenite, which at the time was imported from Cartagena, Spain. How else could one explain its unique and haunting natural luminescence? King Minos of Minoa constructed the walls of his sacred palace from selenite for this reason. When the full Moon's light flooded the palace, the walls appeared to glow from within, as if to cast heavenly approval on the monarch. Centuries later, in ancient Rome, Pliny the Elder published *Natural History*, about the magical and mundane uses of gemstones. He describes the wealthiest of Roman citizens, including Roman Emperor Tiberius (42 BCE–37 CE), as building structures adjacent to their luxurious homes called "specularis," early forms of glass-enclosed greenhouses, which featured beds of stone on wheels that could be moved outside during summer and inside during winter to protect plants from frozen temperatures. Wealthy Romans built specularis from selenite, referred to in ancient Rome as *specularis lapis*—*lapis* simply meaning stone, and *specularis*, the ability to see through. While regular citizens built specularis from glass, the elite chose crystal—presumably for its magical and ethereal powers drawn directly from the Moon. When the Sun passed through the quartz and mica windows, heat was magnified and plants grew miraculously strong. Emperor Tiberius enjoyed gardening and working with nature's cycles, enhancing them with the magical properties of crystals.

TOPAZ

Topaz is a crystal with a long lineage whose roots begin in ancient Greece and Rome. The name *topaz* comes from *topazos*, the ancient Greek name for a small island off Egypt's southern coast called Zabargad. While Zabargad never produced topaz, it was once a source of a light yellow-green stone the Greeks and Egyptians referred to as topaz, but was actually peridot or chrysolite. In fact, Zabargad is where Cleopatra sourced her peridot. Another plausible theory on the origin of the name topaz is that it derives from the Sanskrit word for fire, *tapaz*. Many at the time believed all topaz was yellow-orange or fire-colored, not knowing it can be found in multiple colors from ice clear to blue, pink, orange or imperial, yellow, and champagne brown.

The Indian origins hint at the association between topaz and the planet Jupiter, which was widely discussed in Roman times. Ancient Romans crowned Jupiter their god of the Sun, and, thus, topaz became associated with solar and fire energies. Romans also believed topaz was a truth-telling stone, revealing the truth in difficult and obscure situations. Topaz was rumored to change color and become darker in the presence of deception or poison. Greeks favored topaz for protection in battle, believing the crystal enhanced physical strength and also made the wearer invisible to enemies. Topaz could hide not only your position but your footsteps, making it difficult to track soldiers or follow them.

ACCESSING CRYSTAL WISDOM: ANCIENT GREECE AND ROME

If you want to work with the magic of the crystals of ancient Greece and Rome, gather two to four stones from those identified in this chapter that speak to you. Hold one or two in each hand. Sit comfortably with your legs crossed and your spine straight, bringing your attention to your breath. Allow yourself to journey back in time. Feel the warmth of the air surrounding you, the marble columns rising high above you. Turn your face to the Sun, and feel its warm rays soothing every muscle in your body, calling you to relax, soften, and enjoy this experience. Perhaps some of your personal magic still resides in these ancient lands. As the door to the past opens before you, step forward and reclaim this ancient part of yourself. It is time, and you are welcome here.

AMBER AND AMETHYST

If you have chosen to work with amber or amethyst, focus your attention on the protection and clarity you desire, for these two crystals are natural magnets for safety and detoxifying, as well as removing low or stuck energies from spaces.

Amber can be placed on your altar or sacred space to cleanse and purify the energies, creating an energetic boundary to prevent the return of unwelcome spirits.

Amethyst is a perfect bedroom crystal because its peaceful frequency induces rest. Amen, A'ho, so it is.

CARNELIAN, OPAL, PEARL, AND QUARTZ

If you have chosen to work with carnelian, opal, pearl, or quartz, focus your attention on where in your life you need passion, courage, strength, or transformation.

If you are called upon to raise the vibration of your space(s)—both physical and energetic—incorporate quartz points or generators into your home décor. You can create a grid for a specific intention with quartz and other gems, or just place one large piece of quartz in the center of your home to raise energy equally accessible from all parts of the house. Extend this energy to the corners of your property by burying a quartz point at the four farthest corners of your property.

Carnelian will help you have more stamina during the day, while pearl will attract wealth and peace.

Opal is a stone of transition and transformation; meditate with it to understand how to work through transitions at work or home, asking for clear guidance about what step to take next. Amen, A'ho, so it is.

SELENITE AND TOPAZ

If you have chosen to work with selenite or topaz, you are called to experience more profound peace and privacy, exposing fewer weaknesses to your enemies. Selenite, in particular, brings the magic of the Moon—including enhanced access to psychic visions—to expand your understanding of how to work with the elements around you. It harnesses the fullness of the Moon to manifest your dreams in real time. Use these experiences to deepen and strengthen your personal faith. Amen, A'ho, so it is.

Chapter 5

CRYSTALS OF AARON'S BREASTPLATE FROM THE BIBLE

Some of the world's most famous crystals are mentioned in the Christian Bible, most notably in the *Hoshen*, or breastplate of Aaron, the high priest. According to Exodus 28, Moses was instructed to inscribe the twelve names of the twelve tribes of Israel on twelve specific gemstones, which were to be laid in an exact arrangement and worn as a breastplate by his brother Aaron, the high priest; this breastplate was a channel of two divine energy streams that allowed for visual communication with God, known as the *Urim*, or light, and *Thummim*, or truth: "Insert the Urim and Thummim into the sacred chestpiece so they will be carried over Aaron's heart when he goes into the Lord's presence. In this way, Aaron will always carry over his heart the objects used to determine the Lord's will for his people whenever he goes in before the Lord." [9] By illuminating or darkening the rows of stones, God communicated his will through the breastplate.

Two main challenges complicate this chapter: stone identification and linguistic translation. Our ancestors were notoriously inaccurate when it came to identifying gemstones. For example, they lumped all blue stones together and called them sapphires, lapis lazuli, or cyanus. As a result, some stones mentioned here may not be what was used in Aaron's breastplate. Moreover, some crystals, such as garnet and beryl, grow in a variety of colors, and our ancestors may not have known that two differently colored crystals were, in fact, the same. Or the stone as they knew it may not translate by name to the same crystal today. Fortunately, we can isolate most of what was likely used.

Learning the breastplate's origins and religious significance is inspirational to people, particularly Christians who feel drawn to crystals but haven't understood their relevance to the Christian tradition or that crystals were, in fact, an early mystical divination tool.

The gemstones in the breastplate were chosen and placed with intention, and their placement is thought to have held deep spiritual and cosmic significance. The breastplate formed a three-by-four grid that looked something like gemstone armor when worn on the body. In this formation, when placed on the high priest, the stones opened a portal to God; when they glowed, victory was at hand, but when dark or cloudy, a negative outcome was anticipated.

Interestingly, the names of the tribes inscribed on the stones may have been a code: The letters forming the names of all tribes also represent the entire Hebrew alphabet, and some even suggest fire was an element used to open portals or doorways to God's spirit.

Whether this is accurate or not, there is at least one stone in each row of gems that represents the fire element or fire energy, either in color or meaning. The twelve gemstones used in the breastplate were also connected to the twelve signs of the zodiac and even aligned to the months

> "The letters forming the names of all tribes also represent the entire Hebrew alphabet, and some even suggest fire was an element used to open portals or doorways to God's spirit.

of the year in later legends. Each row represents the fulfillment or fruition of a certain facet of God's divine light and truth as it manifests in the world and in heaven, honoring the hermetic principle, "As above, so below."

Even the legend of how the breastplate stones were engraved is a magical one that sounds like something out of science fiction. They may have been encoded by the *shamir*, a mystical worm-like creature that could gaze upon any material, including stone, and carve any shape or letters into it. The shamir is said to have later been a gift from a mysterious entity to King Solomon; he used it to construct the first temple in Jerusalem.

How the completed breastplate worked in a literal sense, no one knows, but some legends say the tetragrammaton, or symbol of God, was placed inside—literally or figuratively—and activated holy light codes or sacred channelings in the form of Urim and Thummim—light and truth, respectively. A question or matter of a divisive nature could be put before the high priest while he was wearing the breastplate, and the gemstones would light up in rows to signal divine affirmation or disapproval, allowing one to interpret the subtle messages of the stones as an answer from God. For that reason, Aaron's breastplate has also been known historically as the breastplate of judgment.

The left side of the breastplate (the high priest's right side) included gemstones corresponding to heaven and God's love of truth and light, while the right side (the high priest's left side) included gemstones corresponding to Earth or the celestial bodies, and humanity's expressions of truth and light. The gems were set in gold, which represented God's goodness, and the breastplate was worn over the heart to represent God's love. Some say high-frequency sound vibrations accompanied the lights within the crystals of the breastplate, and the light in the crystals may have been produced by these harmonic, angelic frequencies.

BIBLICAL STONE NAME
Odem
Pitdah
Bareqeth
Nophek
Sappiyr
Yahalom
Leshem
Shebuw
Aclamah
Tarshish
Shoham
Yashpheh

AARON'S BREASTPLATE GEMS AT A GLANCE

MODERN AND HISTORICAL STONE NAME(S)	TRIBE	PLACE OF ORIGIN (Ancient and Modern)
sard, sardonyx, carnelian	Reuben	Africa, Middle East
topaz	Simeon	Brazil, Africa
emerald, chrysoprase, green garnet	Levi	Africa, India
red garnet, carbuncle, anthrax	Judah	Africa, India
sapphire	Issachar	India, Sri Lanka, Burma
diamond, jasper	Zebulun	Africa, Brazil, India
ligure, diamond, lapis lazuli, chrysocolla, malacolla, Eilat Stone, cyanus, jacinth	Dan	Africa, Afghanistan, India, Israel
agate	Gad	Africa, India, Middle East
amethyst	Naphtali	Brazil, Africa
beryl, chrysolite	Asher	Brazil, Afghanistan, Africa
onyx, turquoise, malachite, beryl	Joseph	Central America, South America, India, Middle East
jasper, white or clear beryl, jade	Benjamin	Brazil, Africa

ODEM OR RED SARDONYX

The first stone in Aaron's breastplate is odem, which translates to *Adam* and is aligned to red sardonyx, a colored variety of onyx available in steady supply, both today and in ancient times. Sardonyx, or sard, is named for the ancient Turkish city of Sardis, where it was mined. Some accounts suggest odem was, in fact, ruby, but we know at the time Exodus was written, roughly 1400 to 1440 BCE, sard was much more readily available, and it is a much softer stone than ruby, so it's easy to carve. Other accounts propose odem may have been carnelian, which is just a lighter orange color of the same microcrystalline material. Sard tends to be more red and black in color, which aligns with biblical descriptions of odem as a red stone. Red is the color of power, courage, and physical strength, and because odem is also the name of an extinct volcano, fire energy is highlighted in this placement.

One of the energies channeled through the breastplate of Aaron, the Urim, translates to both light and fire; hence a number of crystals in the breastplate have fire associated with them. Some legends say most gemstones in the breastplate were either fire-colored or had flashes of fire within them, signifying the fire of divine truth and light. Fire was also thought to open portals of divine contact through which one could commune with God's spirit and access his wisdom.

PITDAH OR TOPAZ

There is near-universal agreement that the second stone in Aaron's breastplate, pitdah, is topaz, in light brown to golden hues we associate with precious champagne topaz today. It is unclear where it would have come from, and some legends suggest it was instead a golden-green peridot or chrysolite (a form of alexandrite that glows green in natural light). The Hebrew word *pitdah* means to take or secure, but the name could also derive from the Sanskrit word *pita*, meaning "golden."

Ancient people believed golden stones brought long life and prosperity and carried the illumination of God within. Topaz was considered a talisman of protection in ancient times, while chrysolite and peridot were associated with power, strength, and abundance.

BAREQETH OR CHRYSOPRASE | GREEN GARNET

The third stone in the breastplate, known as bareqeth, is Hebrew for "lightning" and was thought to be a description of a fiery flash within the crystal. It is described as a pale green stone with golden or red inner flashes. Most sources agree bareqeth is likely chrysoprase, though some insist it was emerald, which would have been accessible via Egypt in the time of Exodus. Emerald is a soft stone that may crack if engraved, so it's more likely to have been either chrysoprase or green garnets (which would have been accessible via Africa). Our ancestors would likely have interpreted a light within their stone as evidence of its power, perhaps a symbol of God's blessing.

NOPHEK OR
RED (ALMANDINE) GARNET

The fourth stone in the breastplate is nophek, or red garnet. Nophek translates to "anthrax" in Greek and "carbuncle" in English—both references to the deep red color of this mysterious stone, widely accepted today to be almandine garnet. The deadly disease anthrax was so named because it produced black lesions surrounded by bright red inflamed skin; these two colors combined were similar to coal in appearance, and the Greek name for coal is *anthrax*. Almandine garnet is a vibrant cabernet-red crystal that, in good quality pieces, looks lit from within; glowing embers of orange, fuchsia, red, and black flash from every angle of this gemstone. Ancient descriptions of nophek describe it as glimmering like fire in the night.

Almandine garnet may have been accessible in India at the time Exodus was written. Each row of Aaron's breastplate has one crystal that typifies the fire element, and this is row two's. Almandine garnet honors the inner fire of humanity and its connection to the sacred heart of Christ. Carbuncle is also protective of its bearer and was used for its light-bearing properties. Given the breastplate was designed to hold light energy (in the form of Urim), it is no surprise that certain gemstones were included specifically because of their overwhelmingly beautiful inner light—a source of wisdom, inspiration, and, most of all, power.

SAPPIYR OR SAPPHIRE

Sapphire is one of the most precious gemstones on the planet, and so it comes as no surprise it is rumored to have been among the gemstones in Aaron's breastplate, holding the fifth position in the sacred grid. Our ancestors often confused sapphires with other blue stones, so the name of this gem in the breastplate does not ensure a sapphire was used in place of lapis lazuli, for example. We know sappiyr was a blue stone because, in Exodus 24, God appears on a sappiyr stone, which is compared to the color of a clear sky. Only the finest sapphires in the world are this light, bright blue color, though some maintain lapis lazuli was the material in question. Lapis is certainly a softer mineral than corundum and much easier to carve; it measures a 5 on the MOHS, compared to sapphire's 9. Lapis lazuli was also readily available in biblical times and had been used by Egyptian rulers to represent and appease their gods for many thousands of years. Moreover, lapis lazuli was used by the Egyptians to represent spiritual truth—a core tenet of the breastplate; perhaps its creators knew of this lineage of Ma'at, goddess of truth and light in the Egyptian pantheon, and incorporated lapis lazuli as an homage to wisdom, intuition, and interdimensional communication between priests and the gods.

YAHALOM OR JASPER | ONYX

Yahalom comes from the Arabic *halam*, meaning "to smite," and so for centuries people assumed yahalom *must* have been a diamond. After all, what other gemstone can smite, or harm, another crystal? However, because diamonds were not used to cut other materials until modern times, that explanation doesn't make sense.

In Greek, the translation became jasper, though still other legends suggest green onyx could have been used for yahalom; it is a relatively hard stone, so it warrants the reference to strength, and it grows in the subtle shade of green often associated with this stone. Kunz noted the reference to smiting could have been made to denote "the use of engraved onyx for sealing." [10]

Multiple accounts indicate the breastplate's sixth stone was green, further evidence it was onyx, which is mined today in green hues in Pakistan. A final option for yahalom, though less likely, is serpentine; green serpentine or jade would have been accessible at the time and would have been both a durable and an easily carved stone. Green jasper would have been similar in appearance.

But, based on all accounts, light, translucent green onyx would have been the most easily accessible and durable material for this position in Aaron's breastplate. Onyx was also used for the final stone of the breastplate and the two shoulder, or remembrance, pieces that held the breastplate in place.

LESHEM | LIGURE OR AMBER
JACINTH | EILAT STONE

The legends surrounding leshem are the most lively, debated, and incomplete of those surrounding the crystals of Aaron's breastplate. Some scholars have given up trying to identify this elusive material, while others claim it is a blue stone that represents the directing of God's light skyward. The name itself comes from a city in northern Italy, Liguria, where amber was shipped from the Baltic region to Greece in ancient times. This is where some got the idea amber was used in the breastplate. However, amber was likely too soft and rare.

Ancient Greek rumors contend leshem was crystallized lynx urine and that the stone's name was a derivation of *lykos ouron,* meaning white urine; this is presumably why some modern interpretations suggest the stone was gold or amber in color. Other scholars maintain leshem is zircon, based on early references to jacinth or hyacinth, which are alternative ancient Greek names for zircon in gold and brown shades. However, the classical Greek name *Hyakinthos* may have been a reference to modern blue sapphire.

Images of leshem are hard to find, but those that exist feature a granular blue-green crystal that looks a lot like modern chrysocolla or Eilat Stone, the national gemstone of Israel. Ancient accounts may have failed to recognize the importance of chrysocolla and Eilat Stone—both of which could well have been known in biblical times.

SHEBUW OR AGATE

Sources universally agree the eighth stone in Aaron's breastplate
was shebuw, or agate. To some it is the most important stone in the
breastplate; its anagram, a-gate, can be translated to mean a doorway or
portal to higher dimensions of divine awareness.[11] In Hebrew, the word
for agate, *shebo*, means "to flame" and is another reference to fire and the
power of God. Agate was more prized in ancient times than it is today and
was used both as a healing crystal and a source of divine blessings.

ACLAMAH OR AMETHYST

All sources concur the ninth stone in the breastplate is amethyst. Purple quartz, which is of course what amethyst is, was mined in the East before biblical times; however, the largest supply came from Syria at that time. Amethyst was used in ancient Egypt, where it was referred to as *hemag*.

One reason amethyst was chosen for the breastplate may have been its dream-inducing and peace-bringing properties. *Aclamah* derives from the Hebrew word *halom*, meaning "to dream." In biblical times, amethyst was believed to induce dreams and visions. It was also used in ancient Greece for health, detoxification, and peace.

TARSHISH OR BERYL | CHRYSOLITE

The tenth stone in Aaron's breastplate was tarshish, or what is likely known as aquamarine or chrysolite today. Ancient legends describe a dreamy blue-green stone the color of open seas, while others detail a white gemstone with faint green hues. Most likely the crystal in question was chrysolite, a variety of alexandrite and member of the chrysoberyl group of gems, which comes in watery hues of green-gold and light aqua. A yellow variety of jasper called *thehen* would have been another viable option for the breastplate in this position; this yellow gemstone from Egypt was widely available at the time and had been successfully used for carvings and amulets. However, thehen was not as translucent, as many believe tarshish would have been, so aquamarine or chrysolite is the more likely option.

SHOHAM OR ONYX

Onyx may be the most important material used in the breastplate of Aaron. Not only was the eleventh tribal name, Shoham, most likely engraved in it, but the high priest also wore two onyx stones on his shoulders, each engraved with six of the tribes' names, which together were said to be part of the breastplate's activating mechanism. The onyx in this position may have been green in color, similar to yahalom, and was at various points compared to emerald and beryl, which grows in light-green shades when chromium levels are high. Still others maintain shoham must have been turquoise, which was popular at the time and readily accessible in neighboring territories—though not in the light green shade necessary.

Onyx is the most likely option and is considered a talisman of spiritual strength and wisdom even today, which would explain why it was used. Rabbi Shohama Harris Weiner explains the letters of shoham are "shin-hey-mem," the initials of Solomon in Hebrew.[12]

King Solomon received the shamir as a gift and was, of course, the first ruler to build a temple in Jerusalem. By looking at the Hebrew language as a code, we come closer to an accurate understanding of the deeper esoteric meaning of the breastplate. Solomon's name and his legacy give us more clues about the materials used in this part of the breastplate, which represents his power, strength, and spiritual leadership.

YASHPHEH OR JASPER

The twelfth and final stone in the breastplate of Aaron is generally agreed to be jasper. Jasper grows in a variety of colors and, in ancient times, a bright and beautiful green shade was commonly accessible. We know white, orange/red, and green/blue stones were preferred for those used in the breastplate, ostensibly for their alignment to the four elements; as mentioned earlier, fire was considered the most sacred element to God and was privileged in the design. Some sources maintain white jasper, not green, was used in the breastplate, though this could easily have been confused with white shades of onyx, also mined in the region during biblical and ancient times. The mutual popularity of green jade and green jasper at the time also led to confusion between those two stones.

ACCESSING CRYSTAL WISDOM: GEMSTONES OF THE HIGH PRIEST

Because the properties of the breastplate stones are not mentioned in the Bible, we are left with modern interpretations of their meanings; however, modern metaphysical meanings are often informed by history, so some may also have been relevant in ancient times.

AGATE

Long considered a **master healer of the mineral world**, agate attracts peace and calm to the bearer and helps overcome depression and anxiety. Work with agate to calm and center your mind, helping you focus and feel more optimistic. Sleeping with agate promotes deep rest and dream recall.

AMETHYST

Amethyst is the peace-bringer, a crystal known for its **detoxification** and **healing** properties. Amethyst heals the spirit and the auric field and can be used to remove low or dark energies from one's energy field. Used before drinking wine, it has been historically rumored to prevent intoxication.

BERYL

Beryl comes in many forms and colors, each with its own healing and transformational properties. Blue beryl or aquamarine is an **emotional healer**, helping one tap into one's deepest emotions and find the root cause of suffering. Yellow beryl or heliodor offers **optimism**, **youthfulness**, and **vitality** to one who wears or works with it. Green beryl is emerald, which brings **wisdom** and **loyalty**, especially in love.

CHRYSOLITE (ALEXANDRITE)

Chrysolite is a light-green crystal known today as *chrysoberyl*. When the crystals are darker and exhibit color-change properties, they are known as *alexandrite*. Chrysolite historically was thought to bring **power** and **prestige** and enhance **physical health** and **strength**.

CHRYSOPRASE

Chrysoprase is a healer of the heart space, helping you connect with infinite supplies of compassion and love. Chrysoprase **supports cardiac health** and also provides a centered peace for those who wear it. Energy streams of renewal, regeneration, and resurrection are associated with this lemon-lime–colored gem.

GARNET

Garnet is **grounding** and **protective** as well as **nurturing** and **supportive**. Garnet has a maternal energy that connects you with your blood lineage. Garnet provides motivation to overcome obstacles in your path to evolution and enlightenment.

JACINTH

Jacinth, known today as *zircon*, is a red-brown stone that, in ancient times, was thought to cure everything from madness to a stubborn cough. Jacinth was also said to bring **health**, **wealth**, and **happiness**, especially if worn in jewelry or sacred adornment.

JASPER

Jasper **attracts loving kindness** to the bearer and encourages self-love, self-expression, and self-mastery. Jasper is a stabilizing stone that supports all physical body systems. It also offers emotional stability, helping you manage emotions without overreacting to external stimuli.

ONYX

Onyx is a stone of **stability**, **strength**, **power**, and **protection**. It cleanses and purifies the aura, repelling dark energies. It alleviates fear and anxiety, which stabilizes and strengthens the central nervous system. Onyx also supports strong decision making.

SAPPHIRE

Sapphire brings **wisdom** and **integrity**, deepening perception and intuition. Sapphire helps you translate hidden messages in your life so you can integrate the knowledge you gain through experience. Sapphire was known to bring great wealth and prosperity in ancient times.

SARDONYX

Sardonyx is a stone of fiery wisdom and personal power that helps you **ground and embody your desires** and **manifest your personal goals** through productive action. Sardonyx offers a steady foundation on which to build your future and helps you channel strength in times of adversity.

Chapter 6

CRYSTALS OF INTERDIMENSIONAL AWARENESS

Many empaths and channels are discerning intense shifts of energy on our planet—intense enough they're even noticeable to those not usually sensitive to energetic changes. Old methods of approaching human problems are no longer effective; Gaia is purging herself of energies that no longer serve the collective highest good. She purges through natural events including floods, dramatic lava flow, and wildfires. She speaks in elements and uses the crystalline grid within her womb to ground, transmute, and raise frequencies that bring healing, purification, and transformation. Earth is her medicine cabinet, overflowing with plants and minerals many believe hold the keys to healing all who suffer. Humans simply need to download and activate the wisdom about how to use crystals. That work is happening consciously and subconsciously, around the world, right now.

This chapter explores the twelve crystals known as the Synergy 12 configuration (azeztulite, brookite, danburite, herderite, moldavite, natrolite, petalite, phenacite, Satyaloka quartz, scolecite, tanzanite, and Tibetan tektite), a name coined by Robert Simmons and Naisha Ahsian in *The Book of Stones: Who They Are and What They Teach* to describe the amalgam effects of working with them collectively. Also discussed here are crystals such as angelite and labradorite that help you open pathways to new energy streams associated with ascension, manifestation, and evolution. Taken together, these are crystals of expedited spiritual evolution—a fast-track pass to soul growth. What Simmons and others have discovered is the power of synergy in crystal healing; by working with certain crystals together, their energy becomes more intensely magnified. A certain alchemy exists between them that even cynics have acknowledged as a buzzing or intense vibration one can feel, especially in the hands and feet, when in their presence. Some minerals, such as angelite, are compatible with the Synergy 12, while others seem to offer no aggregate benefit when added to the mix. It is best for the practitioner to experience these crystals personally, to sense one's individual resonance with them. The Synergy 12 stones are now quite expensive, but even tiny pieces can be used to harness their effects.

The crystals in this chapter are *gateway crystals,* portal openers to the fifth dimension of awareness and beyond. In the fifth dimension, energies collapse in on each other, time folds in on itself, and the past and future become available to you now. Each crystal has a message for you about how to release your grasp on what you think you know in order to allow the universe to reveal what you are ready to see and receive. By working with them, you will become lighter and more open to divine possibility. Becoming aware of other dimensions allows you to see your daily challenges from an elevated place of understanding and peace, putting your struggles in perspective.

In Eastern traditions, it is common to talk of human life as a waking dream wherein we co-create identities and work through blessings and trauma to heal, grow, and evolve. If this life is a dream, the crystals of interdimensional awareness are your guides and translators. Let them become beacons of clarity and hope, optimism and joy. It is critical for you to acknowledge there is more to this universe than you can see. Once you believe your human life is "all there is," great sadness and despair arise. When you believe in something *or someone* greater than you, a force capable of sacred creation, you'll experience a peace unshakable by human forces. Ascension is your key to lasting happiness.

CRYSTALS OF INTERDIMENSIONAL AWARENESS AT A GLANCE

CRYSTAL	PROPERTIES	PLACE OF ORIGIN (Ancient and Modern)
Angelite	angelic contact, peace, mindfulness	Peru, United Kingdom, Egypt, Mexico
Azeztulite	power, channeling, spiritual growth	United States
Brookite	connection across dimensions, unity consciousness	United States
Danburite	healing, psychic surgery, removal of energetic blocks and unwanted energies	Mexico
Herderite	development of psychic gifts and abilities, contact with spirit guides	Brazil, Germany, Pakistan, United States

CRYSTAL	PROPERTIES	PLACE OF ORIGIN (Ancient and Modern)
Labradorite	new Moon intention setting, visioning, new beginnings	Madagascar, Australia, Russia
Moonstone	full, fruition, goddess energy, and feminine empowerment	India, United States, Brazil
Natrolite	healing of subtle body systems, balancing of hormones and frequencies	India
Petalite	protection, psychic boundaries	Brazil, United States, Pakistan
Phenakite	manifestation, transformation, and transmutation	Africa, Russia
Satyaloka quartz	spiritual healing, acceleration of spiritual development	India
Scolecite	flow of light energy, dream interpretation, channeling	India
Tanzanite	spiritual protection, alchemy, transformation, and manifestation	Africa
Tektite	communication, especially between lovers; chakra clearing and healing	China

ANGELITE

Angelite, a form of anhydrite, is the crystal of the angels. In Greek, *anhydrous* means "without water." Angelite is a very soft stone measuring just 3.5 on the MOHS, and its softness is part of its charm. Calming to the touch and soothing to the energy field, angelite invites a deep state of conscious awareness from which one can attune to higher angelic frequencies. By holding angelite and calling in your guardian angels and spirit guides, you attract energies of peace and protection. Much meaning has been made both of the location in which angelite was first found, near Machu Picchu in Peru, and the timing of its discovery on the eve of the famed 1987 Harmonic Convergence organized by José Argüelles. Some believe angelite was gifted by star beings during the convergence as a sign of the new age, in exchange for human willingness to organize the first global, synchronized meditation event. People gathered all over the world, by the thousands, at vortex locations and other sacred points to share the experience and energy of the convergence. Argüelles was planning another convergence to honor the 2012 stargate when he passed away. In many ways, angelite represents his mission to spread harmony, truth, and light across our planet. When working with angelite, you can still connect to the frequency of the convergence, which through interdimensional awareness is active and accessible today.

AZEZTULITE

Azeztulite is a golden form of quartz discovered by Robert Simmons after a premonition by *The Book of Stones* co-author Naisha Ahsian that an entity called Azez would be activating pockets of quartz crystals around the planet to align with a powerful light energy source. To date, several pockets of azeztulite have been discovered in the United States and South India. Simmons claims it is aligned with the "light of the central Sun" and can easily dissolve fears, helping you overcome bad habits and old ways of being that no longer serve you.[13] He encourages others to communicate with pockets of quartz within Earth, from wherever they are, and to align with Azez frequencies. In this way, we can all attune to and activate quartz to connect with the broader matrix of the azeztulite field and expand the footprint of this interdimensional ascension tool.

You can program quartz to hold a specific frequency or resonance in alignment with your intention. Thus, it can be programmed to align with Azez or any other energy. When unprogrammed, quartz aligns to the dominant vibration in its environment. Within the Synergy 12, azeztulite is the bringer of embodied peace. By working with azeztulite, you activate the physical manifestation of your healing lineage, and your unique soulprint emerges using whatever modality you have been called to master in this lifetime. When working with azeztulite, pay attention to even the subtlest signs.

BROOKITE

Within the Synergy 12, brookite is the bringer of unity consciousness. Brookite is encoded with the hermetic principle, "As above, so below," which represents the divine balance of cosmic forces in the universe. Brookite encourages one to go within and find a holy sanctuary of inner stillness and silence. From that place, it is easy to connect with the frequency of the Holy Spirit or unity consciousness. Expressing itself as a talisman of oneness with life force energy, brookite is a master healer of all body systems and can help the bearer or wearer detect the origin of disease in oneself or a client.

Brookite grows within and is often found with clear quartz, which magnifies its healing and integrating properties. Use brookite during times in your life when you must trust the process, allowing events to unfold in alignment with your highest good and tolerating ambiguity in service of spiritual growth. If you seek greater peace in the outside world, you must recognize you are simply a mirror of all that faces you in the world. Peace without you begins as peace *within* you. Also remember to rely upon your soul family in this time. If people want to connect with or be of service to you at this time, allow the connection and trust its authenticity.

DANBURITE

One of the most beautiful and intriguing of the Synergy 12 gemstones, danburite's primary skill is energetic and karmic healing. Danburite is the psychic surgeon of the Synergy 12, allowing you to pierce the heart of a concern or problem, instantly understanding and healing not only its root cause but also its deeper anchors in your family line.

Originally found in the United States, most danburite today comes from Mexico, though there are pockets in Africa as well. If you have healing to do from your past, or work to do on behalf of an ancestry that has not yet found its way to healing light, this stone is for you. Wearing danburite helps you remember and inspire others to do this sacred work, almost like a bindi functions as a reminder for the wearer to pray. It also elevates your personal frequency to align to universal light and healing energy streams, like driving onto a highway of healing energy. Tapping into this endless well of healing light, which is your birthright to access, allows you to locate and restore lost soul fragments shed during traumatic experiences. For this reason, danburite is a favorite among shamanic practitioners and those who facilitate soul retrieval and integration. Danburite deepens states of consciousness in meditation, so if you find you have trouble letting go or dropping in during meditation, try using it as a crystal ally for this work.

HERDERITE

Herderite is the master teacher and channel of the Synergy 12, the deepest well of intuitive wisdom; it is the seat of knowing and learning. Herderite opens, aligns, and balances the third eye and crown chakras, helping you connect with spirit guides and opening pathways to mediumship capabilities. To use herderite effectively, you need the balancing energies of the other eleven stones in the Synergy 12 formation, which focus the energies of Herderite in specific directions to help tap into the wisdom needed for a given person or circumstance. Herderite is like the universal librarian, holding all the keys to all ancient and stored wisdom. It can only be helpful if you have a question or know what you are looking for. Once directed in a productive way, the energy of herderite brings impressive acceleration of spiritual gifts including deepening the five primary clairabilities: clairaudience (clear hearing), clairsentience (clear feeling), clairvoyance (clear sight), claircognizance (clear knowing), and clairalience (clear smelling).

MOLDAVITE

Moldavite is not so much a crystal but crystallized molten glass formed via a collision between a meteor and Earth more than fifteen million years ago. Some metaphysical practitioners prefer not to work with moldavite because they believe it carries residual extraterrestrial frequencies that cannot be cleared or transmuted. For most, that residual energy is precisely the draw of moldavite—it represents the vast unknown, holding wisdom and answers to questions we have been asking for thousands of years. Moldavite represents interdimensional alchemy, the striking of a match and the flame of connection between two heavenly bodies.

In the Synergy 12, moldavite is the accelerator; it expedites the flow of energy and ideas, helping manifest thought into form. Moldavite accelerates personal human development as well, and people sometimes say they have a hard time keeping up with it. Moldavite will push you until you may want to wave the white flag of surrender. It will teach you what your borders and boundaries are and how far you really can go before you reach your deepest capacity for love. As a heart chakra material, it also accelerates a soul's development in love, often fast-tracking the arrival of a soulmate into the bearer's life. One should be conscious of divine timing and surrender personal will if using moldavite to attract soulmate love.

LABRADORITE

Labradorite is the primary crystal of the new Moon, when we lack the Moon's direction and must rely on our own intuition. It's not a member of the Synergy 12, but it accelerates spiritual growth and development. Labradorite helps focus your thoughts on your deepest desires and intentions and creates space for source communication.

An Inuit legend tells, once, long ago, the northern lights fell from the sky. An Inuit warrior tried to release them by striking the stones with his spear, but some remained trapped, which is why labradorite glows in a range of colors. One can meditate by gazing into the flashes of fire within labradorite. These color rays are a form of communication between you and the source.

- The red ray represents the root chakra, stabilizing and grounding your energy.
- Orange represents passion, illuminating the sacral chakra.
- Gold symbolizes the solar plexus chakra and your power center, reminding you of the strength of your will.
- Light green activates the heart chakra, opening you to expanded sources of love and connection.
- Blue aligns with your throat chakra to help you speak your truth with conviction.
- Indigo exposes you to new channels and sources of wisdom.
- Violet opens your crown chakra to connect you with God's spirit.
- Rose-colored flashes are angelic glimmers of hope and illumination from the soul star chakra, softening your heart and embracing you in the flow of divine feminine love held by divine masculine protection.

MOONSTONE

Moonstone is not a member of the Synergy 12 but is in this chapter because it is the counterpart to labradorite, holding lunar energies associated with growth, fullness, and fruition. Moonstone, in any color and form, represents birth, completion, celebration, and manifestation. Just as you should work with labradorite at the new Moon to anchor new intentions for the lunar cycle ahead, so, too, should you work with moonstone at the full Moon to honor and express gratitude for the gifts you have been given. This authentic gesture of gratitude begins the cycle of abundance, allowing energy to flow toward your newest desires.

Moonstone is a crystal of feminine optimism and regeneration, a sacred reminder that what is empty can become full again. In India, moonstone is associated with the goddesses of the Hindu pantheon and represents mystery, sensuality, and the watery cycles of nature. The flash and fire within rainbow moonstone represent phoenix energies of regeneration and rebirth. Meditating with moonstone helps you reflect on your path, feeling gratitude for the lessons you have learned and the great wisdom you have integrated. It also helps you connect with your matrilineal healing gifts, honoring your abilities and their roots in the women who came before you.

NATROLITE

Natrolite is the great cleanser and activator of the Synergy 12 group. Energetically, natrolite is aligned with the human central nervous system, where it monitors and relays energetic messages. A member of the zeolite family, a master healing configuration of crystals from India, natrolite facilitates contact with the higher self, or master inner teacher—the part of ourselves that knows best how to embody one's deepest truth.[14] Natrolite naturally activates dormant wisdom and light codes as they are needed in one's life. As a result, wisdom naturally seems to flow through this mineral, and crystal healers from around the world stockpile it.

To ascend spiritually, one must raise an immense amount of energy. This requires mental, emotional, and spiritual fortitude. Natrolite is an ally in the energy-gathering process, helping strengthen your spiritual reserves. If you are a healer or empath, natrolite is an important healing tool to keep in your crystal collection. In metaphysical circles, natrolite is used to help heal physical conditions that affect the central nervous system, in particular the myelin sheath surrounding nerves. Those with Multiple Sclerosis and degenerative brain disease have turned to natrolite in recent years as one part of a holistic treatment protocol. By focusing attention and intention on healing through movement of stuck energy, natrolite helps promote positive energy flow through both the physical and subtle bodies. Natrolite also helps empaths maintain good auric boundaries during healing work.

PETALITE

Petalite is the grand protectress of the Synergy 12, the white velvet cloak of protection. When working with petalite, one feels a deep sense of peace and trust that everything is unfolding in perfect time and divine order. Petalite offers this peace and connection as its gifts. Once you settle into an abiding trust in the universe and surrender the driver's seat, events and inspiration unfold easily. Manifestation occurs spontaneously. Petalite protects you gently while you move into this space of divine unfolding, almost like a mother protects her child. Within this energetic womb, you have support to explore your dreams and desires. Petalite can be used to create a protective grid for your space, or it can be used to create a protective gemstone elixir.

Petalite is also an ideal stone to use for amulets or talismans of protection; it can be worn easily by almost anyone and is very attractive. Many metaphysical practitioners prefer petalite over some of the darker, heavier protection crystals, such as black tourmaline and hematite. It's protective but not overbearing or overgrounding. When one is overgrounded, one feels a sense of hyperawareness of circumstances and takes in information through fewer channels, engaging less of their intuitive capacity. Petalite is good medicine for this exact circumstance. It lifts you up and helps you trust, surrender, let go, and listen for guidance from the spirit, not just the wisdom, of this world.

PHENAKITE

Phenakite is a recent discovery to the metaphysical community. Its name comes from the Greek word *phenakos* or "deceiver," because it looks deceptively like quartz. Not only does it facilitate manifestation as the creative agent of the Synergy 12, but it can spontaneously attune other crystals, most notably quartz, to its frequency. As a transmitter of high-frequency energy streams, phenakite facilitates psychic development. It accelerates personal spiritual development and deepens shamanic journey experiences.

Phenakite also helps one integrate the wisdom gleaned through advanced spiritual work, bringing one's wisdom into daily practice, which, of course, makes life better, easier, and more productive. Humans are only limited in terms of what they can accomplish by the breadth of their imaginations; we stop ourselves from evolving, perhaps because on a subconscious collective level we realize we are not prepared for a full-scale ascension movement yet.

Phenakite is one of a new tier of crystals emerging from Gaia's matrix to help us push past our personal obstacles, which become collective obstacles. One crystal, one person, and one action at a time, the planet awakens. By harnessing this power to overcome what has limited us in the past, phenakite is fast becoming a favorite manifestation crystal. Some of the mining locations of phenakite are on or near vortex places of energetic power, which contributes to public fascination with this magical mineral.

SATYALOKA QUARTZ

Satyaloka quartz helps purify one's energy field by facilitating the release of stored energies that no longer serve. It carries a vibration of spiritual healing and evolution and, like phenakite, can accelerate a person's individual spiritual evolution. What makes Satyaloka quartz special and rare is its mining location—it comes from the Satyaloka monastery in southern India.

Its unique markings or etchings differentiate it and make it possible to distinguish Satyaloka from other, more common, forms of quartz. Legends say, at one time, the most enlightened beings on Earth gathered and lived in Satyaloka. In Sanskrit, *Satyaloka* means "realm of truth." The monks who live at Satyaloka monastery gather the quartz pieces and bless them. They believe by sharing this quartz with the world, they raise human consciousness and help people achieve accelerated enlightenment. Satyaloka helps you erase, or clear, old codes and programming that might be holding you back from achieving enlightenment and liberation from suffering. In the Synergy 12, Satyaloka quartz functions as a remover of obstacles to growth.

SCOLECITE

Scolecite is one of the most powerful stones of interdimensional awareness because it functions like an antenna—sending and receiving information from other realms. Scolecite carries the Om vibration, the sound of the name of God, and instantly brings peace and deep relaxation to those who work with its delicate form. In the Synergy 12, it functions like a giant beacon of light, allowing the rest of the stones to express their fullest illumination as well. Scolecite helps you connect with the voice and wisdom of your highest self, the most authentic and true version of your core essence. When you feel disconnected from your higher self, you can feel lost, confused, and despondent. By meditating with scolecite, you strengthen your connection to this voice of inner wisdom and knowing.

Scolecite, and another member of the zeolite family called *stilbite*, are excellent channels of dream-state wisdom. By holding this stone before bed and setting an explicit intention to remember your dreams, you will have a much easier time understanding and interpreting the messages you receive during sleep. To maximize this work, keep a small journal near your bedside and write down any dream memories immediately upon waking. You might keep a small piece of scolecite on top of your journal as you sleep, to infuse its pages with the energies of recollection, receptivity, peace, and integration.

TANZANITE

Tanzanite is one of the rarest crystals on the planet, found only in one sacred place: Mount Kilimanjaro. The Masai people were the first to find the tiny blue crystals scattered across their land after a massive thunderstorm. As the legend goes, sometime in the 1930s lightning struck the Merelani Hills and a massive fire ensued. The people fled; when they we returned, they found and gathered the sparkling indigo gems from the ground, keeping many, sensing they might hold value. They referred to these magical crystals as gifts from the fire in the sky, or lightning bolt.

One Masai elder shared the crystal with a local prospector named Manuel D'Souza, who had been looking for rubies and sapphires in local areas. D'Souza first thought the tanzanite crystals were sapphires, but some of tanzanite's most striking features, including its trichroic inner fire and unique termination, suggested this was an altogether different mineral. D'Souza shared samples with geologist friends, who eventually shared them with executives at Tiffany and Co. in 1967. From there the world was introduced to one of it rarest and most treasured gemstones. Mining efforts began to determine whether more tanzanite lay under the surface, and pockets of tanzanite were found below the Masai land, near the Merelani Hills. Today the mining industry in Tanzania supports an entire sector of the country's economy.

Tanzanite's alchemical and spontaneous origins and rarity contribute to this crystal's wild popularity in metaphysical circles. Tanzanite is the result of a geological anomaly that occurred more than 550 million years ago when two tectonic plates collided, producing massive heat that melted the rocks, forming an alchemical collision of minerals not previously united. The result is a rare blue-violet color with flashes of copper and fuchsia unrivaled in the mineral world. Much meaning has been made that tanzanite was formed of fire and then discovered when fire struck Earth. Local people believe this fiery gem came to them as a gift and message from the gods, to bring and restore hope, prosperity, and power to the region.

In the Synergy 12, tanzanite is responsible for regeneration and the raising of energy. Tanzanite facilitates spontaneous creation and flow of energy, almost like a fountain of light. Meditating with tanzanite, especially in your right hand, allows you to tap into this flow of luminous energy; feel it rise within your fingertips, moving through your veins and over your skin, up and over your shoulders, and then down your left arm. Send the energy from your left fingertips and direct it anywhere you wish to experience this strong frequency of light. As you do, imagine the blue-violet flame rising within you, supporting you, encouraging you, empowering you. Stay with this energy stream as long as you like, and enjoy the grounded peace it brings.

TEKTITE

Tektites, or Tibetan tektites, come from China and Tibet and are revered there as sources of wisdom and spiritual power. Tektites were first mentioned in China around 900 BCE. They were referred to as *agni mani*, or fire pearls, as well as stones of the fire gods.

The predominant theory of tektite's origin is they are the result of a meteoric collision with Earth, and so carry extraterrestrial information. Its unique origins may have something to do with its special powers. In Tibetan legends, the *cintamani*, or mani, stone is a wishing stone, one of four items said to have fallen from a supernatural chest from the sky carrying items that brought dharma to Tibet. On it was inscribed the mantra *Om mani padme hum*, which is said to contain all of the Buddha's teachings. It may carry the secrets of the universe.

Healers use tektite to open and align the chakras. If lovers are to be separated, they should sit together with a pair of tektites, sometimes called the long-distance relationship crystal, in meditation. If they hold the two tektites together, with both their hands touching both pieces, the stones will form an energetic connection through which they can communicate across space and time.

In the Synergy 12, tektite is the channeler and transmitter. It receives information from the entire astral plane and translates it into usable form. It heals blockages in the energetic field and clears energies unresponsive to other materials.

ACCESSING CRYSTAL WISDOM: GEMSTONES OF THE INTERDIMENSIONAL AWARENESS

These crystals accelerate personal and planetary growth, enlightenment, and ascension. Each opens a different door to heightened states of awareness and consciousness.

ANGELITE

Angelite is a **master healer** of the mineral world. It attracts peace and calm to the bearer and is said to be particularly helpful for overcoming depression and anxiety.

AZEZTULITE

Azeztulite has been activated to **support your fullest potential** and help you activate healing energies within your body. Perhaps you have been asking for more guidance and direction. Azeztulite facilitates strong connection with spirit guides and teachers on the Earth plane.

BROOKITE

Brookite **opens divine pathways** for **cosmic communication**. It also helps those who feel like they live between two worlds more easily integrate spiritual wisdom. Brookite is a peace-bringing and peacekeeping stone that helps you embody a vibration of oneness and unity in your daily life.

DANBURITE

Danburite is a healer and a bringer of **divine compassion**. Danburite teaches the healing benefits of compassion, supporting you to become a teacher and role model for it. If you let it, danburite will remove anything not serving you from your energetic field; simply meditate with danburite and ask that it be so. Remember, the peace you seek exists in other dimensions right now, in perfect form. To access it, work with crystals of interdimensional awareness, danburite in particular.

HERDERITE

Herderite helps you **intuit your primary psychic gifts** and can also help you understand how to manifest your gifts in the world.

LABRADORITE

Labradorite **ushers in change** but helps you navigate change with grace. It is a stone of seers and mystics that, when used in scrying, can open visual access to future events. Labradorite sends your new Moon intentions upon the crow's wings, and it's considered the vehicle of preferred transmission for wishes, intentions, and dreams.

MOLDAVITE

Moldavite is a crystal for the advanced practitioner. Moldavite **accelerates spiritual growth** and can fast-track your soul's development. When working with moldavite, hold a strong intention for your work. Many different and unpredictable energy streams are accessed using moldavite; they can be managed through intention and prayer.

MOONSTONE

Moonstone anchors **energies of fullness**, **completion**, and **gratitude**. Such is the energy of the full Moon, where your "meal" is the completion of cycles of life and events between points in lunar darkness. Moonstone symbolizes an answer to prayer, in forms you may or may not immediately recognize or appreciate but are always aligned to your highest good and higher purpose.

NATROLITE

Natrolite brings **healing to the subtle energies** within your body and all around you. It is one of the finer points of early protection, before you can even sense that energies are overwhelming you. It is the shell of your protective egg and can be a powerful tool for empaths and healers, who are more affected by energetic changes than others.

PETALITE

Petalite is a strong protection stone. It is the **white velvet cloak of strength** and protection that helps you move safely in the world without heavy armor. Petalite is every introvert's secret weapon and the key to living peacefully in a harsh world.

PHENAKITE

Phenakite **expedites the manifestation of matter** from pure thought form. It is a crystal that evolves both individual and collective consciousness.

SATYALOKA QUARTZ

Satyaloka quartz **carries divine feminine healing energy**. Reiki masters and spiritual healers use it to access the specific vibration of the monastery where it is found, because this vibration is known to prompt healing and recovery.

SCOLECITE

Scolecite, the **crystal beacon** of the Synergy 12, shines its bright light of illumination on all who work with it. Scolecite activates and clears the upper chakras and supports accurate dream interpretation.

TANZANITE

Tanzanite is a rare gem of **protection** and **inspiration**, an alchemical gift of the gods in Tanzanian legend. It brings a fountain of energy that can be used for healing work, and it strengthens one's spirit ahead of intense spiritual work.

TEKTITE

Tektite is considered a fiery gift of the gods, a result of meteoric collision with Earth. In Tibetan legend it **carries the wisdom of the Buddha** and can align all chakras instantly to facilitate energetic flow in the body. Tektite also facilitates remote healing and communication.

Chapter 7

CRYSTALS OF QUANTUM HEALING

Crystal healing is a buzz phrase in the metaphysical world—so much so one cannot make accurate assumptions about what it actually means. Crystal healing is an entirely relative and evolving arena of energy work with no defined parameters or even agreed-upon tenants. However, crystals are—without question—one of the most important metaphysical access points for healing energy.

I n this chapter, the focus is on a relatively new concept that
acknowledges the multidimensional and complex nature of healing.
Quantum healing can be most accurately defined as healing that
occurs *outside traditional conventions,* even outside third-dimensional
space-time conventions, in deeper states of activated awareness
including theta, gamma, and delta states of consciousness. To reach
these deeper states of presence and activate them, one can work with
crystals, plants, and other medicines—some of which remain guarded
secrets in native cultures. Once you access these tools, parameters of
time and space disappear and you open a door to an entirely new world.
The best part is, you can do this work where you are. Interdimensional
work does not require time travel, only an open mind and tools to
facilitate access.

Quantum healing acknowledges the potential for crystals to serve as
healing tools and transmitters of wisdom, but they are merely *one tool* in
a much bigger toolbox that includes thought patterns, ancient mantras,
essential oils, herbs and plants, sound waves, physical movement, and
sacred geometry. Because this book focuses on crystals, this chapter
focuses on the crystals of quantum healing, including their origins,
legends, and histories. Special emphasis is placed on crystals not
explored elsewhere in this book, some of which have quantum healing
properties of their own.

Most of the crystals described in this chapter are new to the metaphysical
and geological worlds but not to Gaia. As "new" (to us) healing crystals
are discovered, crystal healers begin to attune to their vibrations and
incorporate them with tools they have been using for centuries. This
integration of emergent and established energies is what keeps the
field of quantum healing alive; it reminds us the human and crystalline
energetic fields are vibrant and active, providing us in every moment with
what is needed for healing and peace on our planet right now.

The emergence of tanzanite in the twentieth century is a prime example
of the way Gaia intuitively and spontaneously births the medicine her
children need. Tanzanite had been hidden within Earth for thousands of

years, until one lightning bolt blasted and exposed a mine for humans to discover. The most exciting part of working with crystals for healing purposes is we have no idea what might be found next or what human condition it might support.

Crystal healers and light workers do their best to stay aware and connected to kindred spirits around the world, constantly finding and exploring new crystal and herbal medicines that come forward from the sacred Earth to offer their healing services. This crystalline network is a constant source of wisdom and feedback about what is working on our planet right now. For that is why they, and why *we*, are here.

The crystals are our teachers, and we are proud ambassadors of their wisdom. Like a good teacher, they guide us toward the answers but don't give us the answers—learning requires a stretch beyond the comfortable to reach a new level, a new height, a new awareness. Each crystal described in this chapter is doing its part to guide you, gently but firmly, toward optimal health and integration. Once you heal yourself, you become a living example of healing potential. In this way, we are all crystal ambassadors, teaching just by being.

Ultimately, quantum healing requires nothing other than vibrational work, which by definition is effortless, spontaneous, and invisible. However, those who achieve quantum healing have had to do immense spiritual work to reach such a level of mastery in a human lifetime; it is not obvious where to look for healing, or how to use the tools once you find them. What may look effortless, and indeed *is* effortless for a master, can take decades, even a lifetime, to discover, learn, and embody. If you encounter such masters in this lifetime, spend time with them and learn as much as possible. You may find those who have healed using quantum modalities do not define themselves or identify as teachers or feel the need to teach in traditional classrooms; try to observe their practices and methods because by being and experimenting, they are teaching and leading.

CRYSTALS OF QUANTUM HEALING AT A GLANCE

CRYSTAL	PROPERTIES	PLACE OF ORIGIN (Ancient and Modern)
Aventurine	growth, expansion, and fertility of life and new ideas	India, United States, Africa
Elestial quartz	ancient wisdom, activation of past life wisdom and memories	Brazil, Madagascar, Africa
Eudialyte	central nervous system healing and integration of divine wisdom, balancing of energies within the human body	Russia, Canada
Golden healer quartz	healing the physical body, restoring confidence, maternal energy	Madagascar, Brazil
Herkimer diamond	transmitting and receiving energy, raising personal and planetary vibration	United States
Kyanite	balancing energies and body systems, peace, centering, and transmuting of low vibrations	Brazil, Afghanistan, Africa
Red hematoid quartz	channeling, simultaneous activation of crown and root chakras for sending and receiving energies, remote healing and viewing	Madagascar
Sugilite	physical healing and recovery, immune support, autoimmune recovery, disease prevention and transmutation	Africa

AVENTURINE

Aventurine is the gemstone form of fertilizer—it makes all gardens grow. Everything it touches blooms—people, plants, even sacred spaces. Aventurine is, in fact, green quartz, which partially explains its expansion properties. Quartz, after all, is the great magnifier of the crystal realm. The hidden healing secret within aventurine is fuchsite, a chromium-rich mica that gives aventurine its green color. Fuchsite is known as a crystal that regenerates the life force and is used by crystal healers for cases of serious and long-term illness, where the life force is weakened and depleted. Fuchsite naturally grows with ruby, another crystal that supports regeneration and activation of the life force in terminally ill patients. Aventurine is relatively common and affordable, which makes it a desirable tool among crystal healers.

Grids made of aventurine can help stabilize all body systems, promoting physical healing and recovery after surgery. Aventurine can be applied on the body to support bone density and muscular generation. When placed in the southeast corner of the home, aventurine also attracts wealth and prosperity. The energy stream associated with aventurine is of new growth. Imagine the tiniest bright green leaves on a tree or vine at the beginning of spring, bursting with new life, fearless and seeking only to expand and extend their reach. Such is the fearless growth energy and potential encoded within green aventurine.

ELESTIAL QUARTZ

Elestial quartz is among the oldest forms of quartz on the planet, imbued with the wisdom of our oldest ancestors. Most comes from Brazil, though pockets are found in Madagascar, often growing with other minerals including amethyst and cacoxenite.

Elestial quartz is characterized by "plating," or overgrowth, that looks like scales—it's known in Brazil as *jacare*, or crocodile quartz. Many elestials formed thousands of years ago on or near water; when the water evaporated over time, skeletal quartz formed, trading water pockets for sharp edges of quartz formations. Other elestials trapped their sacred waters within, like a womb; these are the elestial *enhydros*, meaning "water within," we work with today. Each enhydro has at least one visible water bubble. Within the sacred water awaits a healing miracle for the recipient or bearer. If you encounter an enhydro, consider it a gift from the source.

Meditate upon the bubble by gazing at its movement, and ask it to unlock its wisdom for you. Imagine how that water flowed freely in ancient times. What was happening on Earth then, and what medicine awaits you once you learn the answer? Perhaps you were alive and serving as a healing priestess. What wisdom does your ancient self have to share with your modern self? The word *elestial* means "to the stars." Let this crystal take you home to the cosmos.

EUDIALYTE

Eudialyte is a relatively rare stone, originally mined in Greenland but also found in Brazil, Canada, and Russia. The name *eudialyte* comes from the Greek words *eu dialytos*, meaning "well decomposable" because it dissolves in acid. Eudialyte activates the heart and root chakras, and, as a result, has developed a reputation as a crystal for autoimmune healing, which requires deep self-love and self-acceptance. Those who struggle with issues affecting the central nervous system report success when working with eudialyte. It is a calming and balancing crystal that accelerates healing of old trauma, including past-life trauma. For this reason, shaman and medicine people have begun incorporating eudialyte into soul retrieval ceremonies and rituals, where fragments of one's soul shed during traumatic experience are re-integrated and healed. Eudialyte also activates memories of love and can be helpful for those who struggle with memory loss. It activates and heals early memories, in particular, and can be helpful for those healing childhood trauma. And, eudialyte supports those developing their psychic and spiritual gifts, as it opens doors to deeper levels of conscious awareness. By activating alpha and theta brain waves, eudialyte facilitates shamanic journeywork and deep states of meditation for relaxation, healing, and connection with the source.

GOLDEN HEALER QUARTZ

Golden healer quartz gets its color from iron oxide deposits, which add strength to this stone's healing properties. Golden healer quartz is found primarily in Brazil and Madagascar and is well known in metaphysical circles as a self-healing variety of quartz. A rare number of Lemurian quartz are golden healers and are especially prized for their properties of empowerment, strength, and physical recovery. In ancient Lemuria, golden healer quartz balanced energies of the divine masculine with the divine feminine, which allowed for perfect harmony, peace, and health. Today we can use golden healer quartz for the same purpose, allowing it to help us anchor into universal love and healing energies for our well-being and the simultaneous evolution of earth.

By meditating with golden healer quartz, you can call in the divine and sacred balance of masculine and feminine within your body, mind, and spirit. Doing so also calls your chakras and hormonal systems into balance. Because golden healer quartz activates the Golden Ray, it can return your full luminescent power to you. Crystals of the Golden Ray activate the solar plexus chakra, our personal center of will and power. Decide where in your life you need to exercise more balance, power, or will and commit today to harnessing the power of the Sun and the energy of golden healer quartz to support you on your path to divine integration.

HERKIMER DIAMOND

Authentic Herkimer diamonds come from one location in the United States: Herkimer, New York. These naturally double-terminated crystals are extremely clear and are said to be among the purest, highest vibrational crystals on the planet. For this reason, metaphysical practitioners often refer to them as ascension stones capable of accessing higher realms of spiritual awareness. When it comes to healing, this pure high frequency counteracts the effects of disease and illness. Herkimer diamonds radiate their white light of healing energy throughout the physical and auric bodies, illuminating areas of darkness or discoloration.

In metaphysical work, Herkimer diamonds are often used in place of real diamonds because they carry similar energetic frequencies but are, of course, much less expensive.

Much like diamonds, Herkimers represent one's ability to triumph in times of challenge and fear. By lifting your awareness out of the lower chakras and opening the upper chakras, Herkimer diamonds help you shift your perspective and awareness away from physical discomfort, toward a state of perfect peace and divine grace. Meditating with one crystal-clear Herkimer diamond in each hand, eyes closed and legs crossed, attunes you to the highest possible frequencies on our planet at this time. These frequencies are capable of healing the mind, the body, and the spirit instantaneously and permanently.

KYANITE

Kyanite is the great equalizer of the mineral world, constantly seeking balance among opposing forces. It grows in a variety of colors—from orange to green to blue and black. While orange kyanite heals creative blockages, the other colors are better known for their physical and emotional healing properties

- Orange kyanite activates the sacral chakra, enhancing passion and creative energies.
- Blue kyanite heals energetic imbalances and even helps with physical balance issues such as vertigo. Blue kyanite brings all body systems into balance and helps regulate the balance of masculine and feminine energies in the body.
- Black kyanite clears stuck energy and can help cut cords to toxic relationships, places, and spaces. Often, physical illness is the result of sustained exposure to energetic toxicity. By identifying and removing the source of toxic energies in your life, you prevent future health challenges from manifesting.
- Green kyanite balances your emotions, activating the heart chakra and helping heal trauma of the heart, including depression and deep sadness.

By working with all three of kyanite's healing colors—blue, black, and green—you activate energies to balance your home and physical spaces, your body, and your emotions. These three crystals may be the hardest-working of all the crystal-healing allies in your collection; their synergy makes them a potent trifecta of healing magic.

RED HEMATOID QUARTZ

Red hematoid gets its color from iron oxide in hematite, which grows with quartz in this grounding and healing crystal. Red hematoid quartz stabilizes your body, anchoring and centering you. Many empaths work with red hematoid quartz on a regular basis because it is an important counterbalance to the deep psychic and intuitive work they do. The hematite in red hematoid quartz supports good circulation—of blood and energy—in the physical body. Often, disease is the result of blocked energy. Doctors of Eastern medicine address such blocks using acupuncture, among other techniques. Crystals can be used in a similar way to identify and remove energy blockages in the subtle body, which, over time, can manifest in physical symptoms and discomfort.

Meditating with red hematoid quartz can calm anxiety and fears and also boost energetic reserves. Hematite supports your life force, revitalizing and nourishing you from within. It can help you feel safer and more secure; emotional stability is also important when one is recovering from any kind of physical illness or disease. For anyone who has experienced trauma, red hematoid quartz is like a comforting compress. It soothes, strengths, and supports you as you work through mental, emotional, or physical challenges.

SUGILITE

Sugilite is a crystal with a growing reputation for healing and wellness. Like eudialyte, it promotes inner peace and acceptance. Sugilite grows with manganese, a powerful anti-inflammatory healing mineral. In metaphysical circles today, sugilite is often recommended alongside eudialyte and kyanite for anyone suffering from conditions associated with imbalance or central nervous disturbance. Sugilite enhances one's intuition, helping you discern the best course of action for your personal health. The manganese in sugilite is also said to help with pain relief; sugilite is a crystal that healers often place on the body during healing sessions for this reason. Pieces of sugilite that are darker in color have a higher proportional manganese content than the lighter, more evenly purple, pieces.

As a potent crown chakra stone, sugilite is also aligned with energies of peace and connection with the source. Sugilite actively repels negative energy in your environment, which supports the maintenance of healing work. Sugilite cultivates a sense of trust and optimism, helping you feel confident in your body's natural ability to heal itself. If you are a healer, sugilite helps you perform healing ceremonies and ritual without taking on your client's physical ailments as your own. Sugilite does this by activating a protective shield of violet light around you, preventing unwanted energies from entering your sacred container.

ACCESSING CRYSTAL WISDOM: GEMSTONES OF QUANTUM HEALING

Following are modern metaphysical properties of the crystals of quantum energetic healing. Each crystal functions on an energetic level to calibrate and align subtle and physical body systems for optimal health. Working with these crystals activates quantum energies. Open to the possibility of miraculous healing! Wellness is your birthright.

AVENTURINE

Aventurine **helps anything grow**—including your plants, your sex drive, and your business. Everything thrives in its presence. Aventurine also brings good luck for new ventures and has even been said to help students achieve good grades in school.

ELESTIAL QUARTZ

Elestial quartz whispers its **healing secrets of the past**. Trapped within its ancient form lie secrets of healers and priestesses; to activate this wisdom, meditate with this stone and ask your spirit guides to transfer knowledge to you about how to cure and transmute what ails you.

EUDIALYTE

Eudialyte **calms and balances the central nervous system**, encouraging self-love and self-acceptance. By activating both the heart and root chakras, you release trauma and past-life karma. Eudialyte reminds you all is well and you are mentally, physically, and emotionally safe in this moment.

GOLDEN HEALER QUARTZ

Golden healer quartz **restores your power** and helps you activate deep healing from a place of personal will. If it is time to improve your self-care routine or personal habits, golden healer will support your efforts to prioritize your well-being.

HERKIMER DIAMOND

Herkimer diamond is the **highest vibrational crystal** to work with if you are trying to raise your personal vibration. Naturally double terminated, Herkimer diamonds are accurate transmitters of universal wisdom. For remote healing, use Herkimer diamonds to transfer healing frequencies or Reiki symbols.

KYANITE

Kyanite seeks stasis and helps bring your body back into **divine balance** after illness or trauma. Kyanite eases physical symptoms of vertigo or dizziness and supports women as they go through hormonal changes during menopause. Black kyanite instantly clears anything it touches, but it does not need to be cleared itself as it does not hold or store energy.

RED HEMATOID QUARTZ

Red hematoid quartz activates both the root and crown chakras to **open optimal energy flow** within the human body; this energy flow can be used for healing, strengthening, or restoring the physical body after surgery, illness, or trauma.

SUGILITE

Sugilite is a **master healer of pain and inflammation**, due to its high manganese content. It is used in crystal healing to support relief from chronic pain and conditions in which inflammation is present. Sugilite calms and soothes the central nervous system. It eases frayed nerves and is said to help order one's thoughts, easing anxiety.

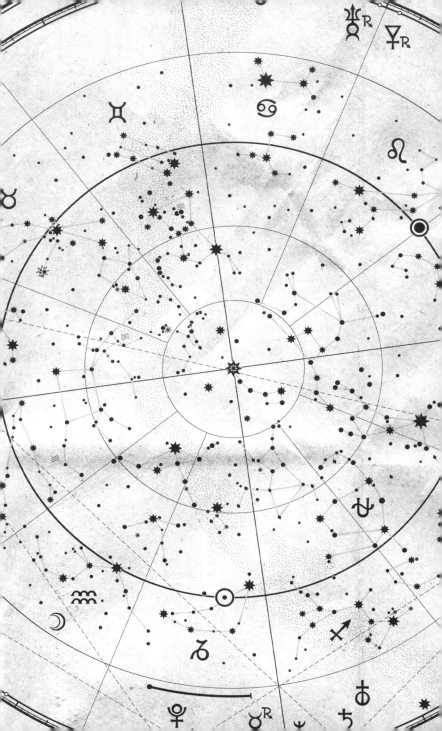

Chapter 8

CRYSTALS OF
THE ZODIAC

Astrology is one of the most popular topics in the metaphysical world and has been for thousands of years. Our ancestors were gifted astrologers who used the positions of planets and stars to help guide their decisions. In Vedic astrology (see chapter 3), gemstones are correlated to planets; in Western astrology, each zodiac sign has both a traditional and an alternate birthstone, or power crystal, assigned to it. These were originally correlated to the twelve crystals chosen for Aaron's breastplate (see chapter 5). In 1912, the National Association of Jewelers issued a comprehensive list of birthstones declaring which gemstones aligned to each birth month. Only a few modifications have been made to the list since.

ecause your birth month only reveals the position of the Sun in your chart, your birthstone represents your *outward* potential, your soul's primary work in this lifetime. Other influences, such as the position of the Moon in your chart, are not represented by your birthstone. When you wear your birthstone or carry it as a talisman, you activate energies to support who you are meant to become.

There are two zodiacal correspondences for each month because Sun signs change every month, at roughly day twenty-one. Whether you are a Capricorn or Aquarius born in January, for example, your birthstone is garnet; the energy of January is about grounding, protection, and stability. The two signs that share a month have some basic influences in common, though their elemental profile is different. For example, Capricorn and Aquarius share a birth month and birthstone, but Capricorn is an Earth sign while Aquarius is an air sign. Capricorn will approach grounding, protection, and stability from an earthy place, adding even more energies of grounding to what is already present in their profile. Aquarius brings air energy and is more likely to activate grounding, protection, and stability from an intellectual place than a physical one. Aquarians often express their protective and stabilizing energies through words rather than actions. Keep this duality in mind as you read each month's birthstone legends. While each month has general energetic themes associated with it, how the signs activate those energies depends largely on their elemental profile.

CRYSTALS OF ZODIAC AT A GLANCE

MONTH	ZODIAC SIGN(S)	BIRTHSTONE (Traditional and Alternate)	PLACE OF ORIGIN (Ancient and Modern)
January	Capricorn/ Aquarius	garnet; onyx	India, Mexico, Pakistan
February	Aquarius/Pisces	amethyst; jasper	Africa, Brazil, India, Uruguay
March	Pisces/Aries	aquamarine; bloodstone	Brazil, Pakistan
April	Aries/Taurus	diamond; quartz	Africa, Israel
May	Taurus/Gemini	emerald; chrysoprase	Columbia, India, Australia
June	Gemini/Cancer	pearl; alexandrite	Russia, India, Africa, Brazil
July	Cancer/Leo	ruby; carnelian	India, Burma
August	Leo/Virgo	peridot; spinel	China, United States
September	Virgo/Libra	sapphire; lapis lazuli	India, Sri Lanka, Burma
October	Libra/Scorpio	opal; tourmaline	Australia, Africa
November	Scorpio/ Sagittarius	topaz; citrine	Brazil, Pakistan
December	Sagittarius/ Capricorn	turquoise; tanzanite	United States, Middle East, Sri Lanka, Burma, Australia

JANUARY

January's traditional birthstone is garnet and alternate birthstone is onyx. The name *garnet* comes from the Latin *granatus,* or "seed," because when mined, garnets look like pomegranate seeds. Garnets are protective, bring stability, and ground you, helping you release anxiety and hesitation. Onyx is similarly grounding, protective, and stabilizing. It supports the skeletal system and strengthens the muscles.

Garnet and onyx both activate the root chakra and the earth star chakra. They bring loyalty to relationships and can ease the pain of separation for lovers. Garnet also helps heal heartbreak of any kind. Physically, garnet is used for detoxification and purification. When placed in a grid formation, garnets can purify and detoxify spaces as well. Most of the world's garnets come from India, especially cabernet-red almandine garnets. Most onyx comes from Mexico and Pakistan. Both crystals are available in a variety of colors and forms, and both are durable choices for carvings or jewelry.

IF YOU WERE BORN IN JANUARY . . .

Your birthstones tell a story of **strength** and **conviction**, a willingness to sacrifice for important causes. You bring strength and elegance to your relationships. You prefer monogamy and predictable routines. You are loyal, reliable, and diligent. You struggle at times to maintain your identity in committed partnerships. Make room in your life for the things and people who bring you joy.

Capricorns activate strength through their physical presence and actions, while **Aquarius** brings strength and stability through words and thoughts.

FEBRUARY

February's traditional birthstone is amethyst. Those born in February may have a gift for self-control. Perhaps they also have the gift of love. Harriet Fobes, in her 1924 book *Mystic Gems*, writes, "The amethyst colors of red and blue, making violet, are symbols of power and light. The deep violet color stands for true and deep love." Amethyst comes in a wide range of purple tones. The deepest, darkest amethysts tend to come from Uruguay or Zambia, while lighter crystals can be found in Brazil.

Aquarius is the sign of universal love, what is known as *agape* in Greek for love for mankind, and represents the ability to love without judgment. February's alternate birthstone is jasper, which grows in a variety of colors. Jasper is the gemstone of loving kindness, which resonates with Aquarian energy of fairness, compassion, and generosity.

IF YOU WERE BORN IN FEBRUARY . . .

Your birthstones tell a story of **love** and **strength**. You are a symbol of peace and balance. You are the essence of power in love, and power through love. You bring out the best in people and tend to experience tenderness in your primary relationships. You also have deep compassion for people who are different from you.

Aquarius activates loving strength through the element of air, using words and thoughts to offer support.

Pisces brings loving strength through empathic expressions of love. Pisces prefers physical affection where Aquarius offers intellectual support.

MARCH

March's traditional birthstone is aquamarine or blue beryl. Aquamarine is a crystal of relaxation, emotional healing, and good luck, especially for travelers. March's alternate birthstone is bloodstone, a green jasper with bright red spots; Christian legends say they come from Christ's blood.

Bloodstone was also known as heliotrope in ancient times; in Greek, *helio* means "sun" and *tropos* means "to turn toward." It could also be named after the flower heliotrope, which, according to legend, is capable of attracting rainfall, or "turning the Sun." It could also refer to the colors of the setting Sun on the waters of the Aegean Sea. Aquamarine and bloodstone are emotional healing crystals that help you get in better touch with your feelings. By processing your feelings, rather than ignoring them, you maintain healthy relationships with yourself and others.

IF YOU WERE BORN IN MARCH . . .

Your birthstones tell a story of **healing** and **emotional support**. You are capable of deep compassion and are here to help and heal others. You have access to a well of infinite wisdom and can use water energy to create flow, through which you bring hope, encouragement, and inspiration.

Pisces heals through empathic touch and communication, allowing others to feel they are not alone. Pisces can also use their imagination to bring new ideas to life.

Aries brings healing through decisive action. Aries inspires others toward change by using emotional intelligence to guide decisions.

APRIL

Diamond is the primary birthstone for April, with clear quartz as the alternate. Both translucent, clear crystals are used to raise energy and strengthen the vibration of a person or place. It is no surprise, then, that April babies are innovators, the first to take action when needed. Aries is the first sign of the zodiac, so this is the natural position of leadership and authority.

George Frederick Kunz tells the story of the origin of the diamond, how God of the Mines commanded his courtiers to bring him "all known gems . . . the ruby, emerald, sapphire, etc." and crushed them together. He then said, "Let this be something that will combine the beauty of all; yet it must be pure and it must be invincible." [15] And diamond was born. The king then said he had created the greatest treasure of the land and, for his queen, he would create the greatest treasure of the sea. And pearl was born.

In ancient times, diamond was believed to cure any physical illness or malady. It was also thought to ensure a lifetime of good fortune, as diamond is ruled by Jupiter, the planet of good fortune; to take advantage of these benefits, however, you must receive your diamonds as gifts. Diamonds purchased for oneself, or worse—stolen, are not believed to have as much power.

Quartz raises your vibration to attract what you desire. Quartz can also be programmed to act energetically "as if" it is any other stone, and so can be programmed to serve in place of diamond for ceremonial and ritual purposes.

IF YOU WERE BORN IN APRIL . . .

Your birthstones tell a story of **power** and **innovation**. You are willing to go first in life, blazing the trail for others who follow. Your judgment is uniquely accurate, and you are successful because you follow it. You make good on your promises and others know they can rely on you for wisdom, direction, and support.

Aries activates this power through interactions with others and innovation of new concepts, projects, and ideas. Aries has faith in their abilities, which inspires trust and faith in others.

Taurus activates this power through manifestation of vision. Taurus creates art in everything they do, and beauty is what they innovate. One of the greatest gift of Taurus is their stunningly accurate ability to translate ideas in physical form.

MAY

May's traditional birthstone is emerald. Its alternate birthstone, chrysoprase, has a similar energy feel and the same hexagonal crystal structure. Emerald has been prized by almost every ruler of every civilization. In ancient times, wearing an emerald on one's forefinger was believed to bring power, because of its connection to Jupiter. Aztec king Montezuma allegedly had a human skull with an emerald pyramid crown. He would pronounce his judgments by touching the skull. Another emerald, the Isabella Emerald, was said to have been "gifted" to Hernán Cortés by Montezuma. Chrysoprase is associated with power as well. Alexander the Great was said to have worn a chrysoprase belt in every battle he won.

IF YOU WERE BORN IN MAY . . .

Your birthstones tell a story of **passion** and **desire**. You commit yourself fully to any endeavor and have the power to manifest your visions. You are creative and cunning, with desirable talents. You inspire others to follow their authentic path, trusting their instincts and pursuing their dreams.

Taurus activates this energy by grounding their passions in art, or expressing it through their work. Taurus sees all projects to completion and creates financial prosperity through commitment and creativity.

Gemini activates this energy through intellectual pursuits. Gemini is a natural-born teacher, gifted with the ability to communicate ideas in interesting ways that are easy to remember. Gemini serves other through their words, sense of humor, wisdom, and wit.

JUNE

Pearl and alexandrite, respectively, are the traditional and alternate birthstones for June. Pearl is a gift of the sea, the result of nature's willingness to persevere and endure hardship with grace. Legends abound regarding its origin: Did it form from a dewdrop? Did God transform tears to pearls? Are they tears of the gods? Regardless, pearls are always associated with water.

Alexandrite is a pleochroic (color-changing) gemstone. It has also mystified collectors for centuries. Discovered in the Ural Mountains, it was named after Russian Czar Alexander II. Some believe its different colors represent different energies and can reflect the mood of the one wearing it.

IF YOU WERE BORN IN JUNE . . .

Your birthstones tell a story of **feminine power** and **royal intrigue**. You have a watery sensibility about you that allows you to move easily and fluidly through any situation. You go with the flow. You enjoy riding the waves and tides of life and you are a very good teacher of how to do that with grace.

Gemini anchors these watery frequencies through their writing, their teaching, or their art in any form. Gemini weaves their wisdom through stories, which entertain and educate.

Cancers activate this watery power through emotions and love, by experiencing and then expressing it. Cancers make any place a home and are natural hostesses, inviting the world to sit at their table.

JULY

July's birthstone is ruby. Cancer and Leo share the month and they share passion, though they experience and express it differently. Ruby is a stone of passion. It is the color of blood, and it supports heart healing. Ruby helps connect you with your deepest desires. July's alternate birthstone, carnelian, does the same work through the sacral chakra, as opposed to ruby's root chakra. They are powerful healers of the lower chakra system, which governs sexuality, passion, creativity, fertility, pregnancy, delivery, and youthfulness. Perhaps this is why queens and empresses of France, Austria, Spain, and England, historically, have worn rubies. Rubies are protective of travelers and, especially, women.

IF YOU WERE BORN IN JULY . . .

Your birthstones tell a story of **passion** and **protection**. You desire to love and be loved. You make decisions based on feelings when you must, because you trust the accuracy of your intuition.

Cancers express this energy by protecting those they love, offering deep emotional service to loved ones. Your deepest passion is to be and create a home for others. You take great pride in your ability to mother others.

Leos activate this energy by taking charge of their lives and becoming a leader at home, at work, or in the community. You look for ways to lead others with love. Your passion is best expressed when you can channel a vision for something and work with others to manifest it.

AUGUST

Stones of cornucopia and prosperity are appropriate for a queen, and because both astrological signs born in August have a queen archetypal association, they are fitting indeed. Peridot is the traditional birthstone for August, and is said to attract whatever you desire. It brings good luck and good fortune to the bearer and was prized in ancient Egypt for this reason. Peridot has been known as the Stone of the Sun, which aligns with its correspondence to August or high summer.

In Hawaii there is one beach where so much olivine, a mineral related to peridot, has washed up onshore it looks like a green sand beach; in reality, the crystals are a byproduct of volcanic activity.

Spinel is the alternate birthstone for August and has historically been mistaken for ruby because, in the right quality and light, it looks deceptively similar. Spinel is associated with the Sun and is a stone of bright enthusiasm and courageous optimism. It brings confidence, which is why it is often associated with manifestation and creation.

Peridot and spinel are complementary stones; peridot attracts plenty of resources while spinel offers courage and energy to use them in service of your highest good. Together, these crystals represent the tenacity and fierce determination of the two Sun signs born in August. Spinel encourages task completion, helping make sure no detail is left unnoticed or incomplete. Spinel also brings stamina and a steady flow of energy to support long-term projects and goals.

IF YOU WERE BORN IN AUGUST . . .

Your birthstones tell a story of **manifestation** and **dedication**, of leadership and self-actualization. You are committed to seeing your plans through from the early stages of formation through to their materialization in the world, and you are careful to make sure the work is done perfectly. To you, love is in the details as well as the big picture and you prefer situations where you can engage both the micro and the macro. You believe more is more.

Leos activate this belief with a sense of extravagance in all they say and do. Leos light up a room like the Sun that rules them, and they bring a childlike optimism to dark spaces. This authentic optimism can be a source of inspiration for many.

Virgos notice all the fine edges of life, and this ability to see what others miss is both a gift and a curse. Virgos find satisfaction in service well performed, especially when that service is deeply appreciated by those who receive it.

SEPTEMBER

September's traditional birthstone is sapphire, a stone mentioned in almost every major spiritual tradition. In Persia, legends say the sky was painted blue using sapphire. According to Birman legend, the goddess Tsun-Kyan-Kse bestowed her sapphire eyes upon Birman, or Siamese, cats when the high priest died following an attack on her temple. Henceforth, monks were destined to live a lifetime as a Siamese cat before ascending to Nirvana.

Sapphire is a teaching stone, helping harness and communicate wisdom with clarity and ease. Sapphire activates the third eye chakra, enhancing insight and foresight.

September's alternative birthstone is lapis lazuli, one of Cleopatra's prized possessions. Lapis lazuli grants power and eternal life. The gold veins represent rivers of prosperity that flow to those who have true power. Lapis is helpful for psychic development.

IF YOU WERE BORN IN SEPTEMBER . . .

Your birthstones tell of **power** and **wisdom**. You are capable of channeling deep wisdom from other realms, and you have an expansive knowledge base. Others seek your advice because you're fair and balanced.

Virgos access power through attention to detail and enjoy exerting control over external circumstances. They believe they can influence the outcome of events and often seem to do just that. A Virgo's mind is a powerful tool.

Libra brings balance to power, helping one discern between the influence of ego versus spirit. Libra prefers power through diplomacy and seeks a win-win resolution in conflicts.

OCTOBER

Opal is a gemstone of hope, optimism, and transformation. It has been prized for thousands of years, though opals have been found in different parts of the world and sometimes look very different depending on mining locale. It's the traditional birthstone of October, which is a transitional month in the northern hemisphere, signaling the winds of change from fall to winter.

The fiery flashes of color burning within opal are meant to symbolize the flashes of hope and optimism alive within you—your inner fire of possibility and faith.

The alternative birthstone for October, tourmaline, is also a stone of possibility and faith. Tourmaline grows in a variety of colors, each with unique metaphysical and energetic properties.

- Green tourmaline brings wisdom in love and engenders fidelity among lovers.
- Pink tourmaline is a heart chakra healer that reminds you it is safe to love again after trauma or heartbreak.
- Golden tourmaline attracts financial prosperity.
- Black tourmaline protects anything it touches from harm.
- Brown tourmaline, known as dravite, is grounding and protective, nurturing and supportive of those who suffer from post-traumatic stress disorder.

Opal and tourmaline are strong allies to use during periods of transition, which happen in every person's life. All events in life unfold in cycles. These crystals honor, recognize, and celebrate those cycles.

IF YOU WERE BORN IN OCTOBER . . .

Your birthstones tell a story of **transition** and **change**; they also tell a story of **triumph** and **possibility** and your victory over challenging circumstances. Those born in October are infused with an otherworldly sense of peace and grace, and they intuitively communicate and share that grace with others.

Libras are known for their smiles and kindness. They activate their gifts through their relationships with others. Of all zodiac signs, Libras are most gifted at understanding and navigating human intimacy. Libra has an intuitive sense of other people's needs and an even more pronounced sense of how to fill them without being overbearing. Libra also remembers to laugh and diffuse stress as a means of reducing anxiety in awkward situations.

Scorpios activate their gifts by analyzing the subtle signs in their environment and using the intense depth of their emotions to hold space for others, channeling deep empathy for the needs of those around them.

NOVEMBER

November's primary birthstone is topaz; citrine, its lapidary doppelganger, is the alternate. Topaz grows in a variety of shades, but golden-yellow is most often identified as the November birthstone. Topaz is rumored to protect soldiers and those in power. It's also been thought to increase physical strength and heal the body when worn in jewelry or burnished into one's armor. Topaz also ensures prosperity and a good harvest.

Likewise, citrine ensures prosperity and is known to attract financial wealth to the bearer.

Both stones activate the Golden Ray of personal power, helping balance and align the solar plexus chakra, your energy center of will and possibility. Citrine releases blockages to prosperity, including energetic blockages from previous lifetimes. Working with natural citrine opens channels to divine abundance and helps you feel worth of prosperity.

IF YOU WERE BORN IN NOVEMBER . . .

Your birthstones tell a story of **wealth** and **wonder**, whereby you rekindle your faith in what is possible.

Scorpios feel entitled to wealth and prosperity, believing financial ease is their birthright. Topaz helps you become physically and emotionally strong, to temper your deep well of feelings that sometimes leads to self-sabotage.

If you are a **Sagittarius**, your warm, bright personality shines like golden citrine or topaz gems. A natural optimist, you inherently possess a wealth of skills needed to attract financial prosperity into your life. Sagittarius tends to prosper financially through acts of service.

DECEMBER

Turquoise is the primary traditional birthstone for December. It, too, has a legacy and lineage that is impressive and truly magical. The finest quality turquoise in the world has always come from Persia, or modern-day Iran, where a turquoise-encrusted Peacock Throne was commissioned by Shah Jahan to celebrate his accession. Equally stunning varieties, such as Sleeping Beauty, have been mined in the United States. Campitos turquoise from Mexico has glimmering rivers of golden pyrite swimming through it. No matter where turquoise is found, it is prized for its qualities of healing, beauty, and harmony.

Turquoise activates the throat chakra to help you articulate your truth with confidence and poise.

Tanzanite is the more recent alternative birthstone for December. Much like turquoise, tanzanite is a crystal known for its healing and transformational energies. Tanzanite emerged from Earth after a violent storm in Tanzania almost 100 years ago. Its crystals are said to bring inspiration for healing, growth, and protection. Tanzanite is a stone of wish fulfillment, the fruition of dreams held silently in the heart for many years.

Those born in December are dreamers and visionaries not afraid to imagine new worlds of possibility seemingly beyond human reach. The birthstones of December represent harmonic ideals of what is possible when people break down barriers and borders that separate them. These are crystals of unity consciousness and spiritual evolution that bring peace, understanding, connection, and planetary healing.

IF YOU WERE BORN IN DECEMBER . . .

Your birthstones tell a story of **harmony** and **healing**. You are encouraged to dream a bigger dream for yourself and your life, through which you can manifest your vision of harmony and unity on Earth. Freedom is critical to those born in December; for your happiness, you must feel liberated and able to move in alignment with your deepest intentions for incarnating into this lifetime.

Sagittarius activates this longing for freedom and harmony by traveling widely and seeing the world, meeting people from all walks of life. By connecting with others and finding shared meaning, you rekindle your faith in humanity as well as your belief in magic. Deep down, all Sagittarians believe magic is real.

Capricorns born at the end of December also retain a childlike sense of optimism about the world kindled by their firm belief in equality. Capricorn is here to succeed in this lifetime, and as they succeed they motive and inspire others to reach their fullest potential.

Conclusion

HONORING AND ACCESSING GAIA'S CRYSTAL WISDOM

Ancient Egyptians believed humans die twice—once when their heart stops beating, and again when their name is no longer uttered by those still alive. Each crystal in this book—and the crystals *not* mentioned here for lack of space—hold a crystallized memory of the development of our planet. If you believe in reincarnation, you are a keeper of these memories, too. You lived once, or maybe many times, hundreds and thousands of years ago in different places across our beautiful planet as these crystals were forming in Gaia's belly. And somewhere your bones from those lifetimes lay buried alongside new crystals forming now, which will be mined and treasured by future generations. The cycles of life, death, and rebirth are never ending.

E very time you work with your crystals, you honor Gaia's wisdom and your ancient knowing. You acknowledge yourself as an emissary of light, here to raise the collective vibration on the planet, and you bow to Gaia, who birthed these sacred tools, each with a unique fingerprint and set of healing codes designed to help us live healthier, happier, and more meaningful lives. Every time you touch a crystal and share its powers, you bring it back to life, helping it reconnect with its life force. What is old becomes new again.

When you read this book and retell the stories catalogued here, you do sacred work to keep Gaia's memories alive for future generations, who, hopefully, will share these tales with their children, and so on.

When you work with a crystal, there are two ways to engage with its stored wisdom—one passive; the other, active.

Just by holding your crystal, keeping it in your sacred space, or meditating with it, you passively connect to its destiny line and energy stream. Passive engagement with crystals brings plenty of healing energy and is a beautiful way to begin working with crystals, especially for a beginner.

But you can do active work with crystals too, allowing them to imprint their unique codes for healing, happiness, prosperity, passion, and beauty into your energy field. Active crystal work requires you to engage your crystals for a focused purpose, ideally in alignment with its inherent frequency. The following meditation allows you to consciously and actively connect to Earth's crystalline grid, the interlocking web of crystal energy that flows across ley lines and through sacred vortex points on our planet where crystals remain implanted, emitting their unique frequencies and communicating with us from beneath our feet. You can use any crystal, ideally a piece of high-vibrational clear quartz, to plug into Gaia's crystalline grid and access the deep stores of energy laying there dormant, waiting for us to find them.

CRYSTALLINE GRID MEDITATION

This meditation is best performed outside but can be done indoors. If possible, get as close to Gaia's outer shell as you can, whether you go to her beaches and move your hands through her sands, or to her forests and place your hands on her trees. If you're inside, just be sure you have access to touch the floor with both hands from wherever you choose to sit or lie down.

Before you begin, smudge with your favorite herbs to cleanse and purify your sacred space. When you smudge, you remove unwanted and stagnant energies from your space and prepare a safe "container" to hold the energies you raise in meditation. Most prefer *salvia apiana*, or white sage, for smudging; it dislodges stuck energies resistant to other forms of clearing or purification.

Once the energy is clear, bring your hands to prayer pose in front of you and bow your head. Take a deep breath in, allowing the air to fill your diaphragm and lungs. Exhale, releasing all the air from your lungs. If that felt good, do it again. Let air flow freely and fully in and out, letting whatever energies come your way find space. In this place you are not resisting, just allowing. Whatever energies wish to leave you, let them go. All is welcome here, but nothing is required. Create freedom for all the energies in your space, trusting that exactly what you need right now is already present. There is no need for anxiety, care, concern, fear, or longing. Here, there is no space for sadness or regret. You are ready, now, and grateful just to be in this moment. So much has been leading you here. Your ancestors bow before you, acknowledging the difficulty of your journey and the grace with which you have walked the road that led you to this place.

Everything is so good here, just as it is, right now.

To begin this ceremony of reconnection with Gaia's ancient wisdom and with yours, choose a piece of quartz from your collection. Quartz is the best material to use because it is programmable and easily absorbs energetic codes from surrounding environments, and even people, including those who lived before. Hold it in your left hand and place your right hand on top of it. Close your eyes and set the intention that this quartz will be your guide as you seek entrance to Gaia's crystal maze and her massive underground labyrinth of crystal power. Gaia birthed her crystals in sacred geometric pathways, placing them in sacred correspondence and communication with each other and with all able to discern and translate their messages. Ask that your crystal be given easy and clear access to the rest of the crystal grid within Earth once you place it into the ground. See if any questions come to mind as you prepare for this exercise. Take another deep breath, allowing your body to soften into this moment. There is nothing to do, nothing to be, and nowhere to go. Everything you need is available here in this moment.

Now, place both hands on the floor or ground in front of you, ideally on soil or organic material. Imagine sacred antennae extending out of the palms of your hands, reaching far down beneath layers of soil and time, directly into the crystal kingdom beneath Earth's surface. Take your quartz and trace a circle on the ground around you, clockwise—from directly in front of you to the right and around you and ending where you began. This opens a sacred circle to hold, contain, and support the energy you access.

Next, take your quartz and push it into the ground as deeply as you can, or if you are indoors, make contact with the floor in front of you. As you do so, imagine all the crystals in Earth rising energetically to meet your quartz. See them extending beams of light toward each other, searching for each other, locating each other along energetic lines of love, power, wisdom, history, and truth. Let the crystals connect—brothers and sisters with an innate connection, finding each other across space and time, and transferring codes to heal, help, and hold those in the mortal realm who need and seek their assistance. You are here as an anchor of their energies, holding the space while the crystals communicate.

Direct your attention to the illuminated energy lines being activated beneath you. Ley lines connect vortex points across the planet and around the world, forming waves of synergistic energy that rise to the surface, illuminating the cosmic rays and energizing the chakras of all humans connected to Earth's planetary matrix at this time. Imagine the energy of your quartz anchoring deeply into Gaia's womb. It is common to feel a buzzing in your hands and feet when crystals are returned to

Earth, even when just placing your quartz on top of soil or grass. They know they are coming home, returning to their mother's sacred womb, and often respond with a surge of energetic messages. Give yourself a moment to acclimate to this wave of energy.

Next, focus your attention on the land. Perhaps you live near one of the ancient civilizations or countries mentioned in this book, or maybe you live near a sacred site not mentioned here. Are you close to a burial site or other hallowed space? Even if not, you might receive wisdom from the crystal you choose to implant that surprises you or tells you a story you have not heard before. Remain open to this wisdom; if you like to journal, take time to write down what you sense and feel. Historically, this process has yielded our most profound crystal legends and wisdom. What you learn today might be a story or legend shared by your ancestors many years from now.

Imagine your single piece of quartz plugging into the massive grid of our planet's crystalline web, like a single bulb on a thousand-light string of lights. Let your crystal illuminate itself with the power and energy of all the others, connecting to them and working with them to harness the energy of the entire grid, sending and receiving whatever wisdom seeks to come through you at this time. Some of your crystals have not seen their crystal families in many centuries; make space for this divine reunion.

What do *you* feel as you begin this process? If you feel close to tears or unusually warm, you are having a common reaction to increased energy flow. Allow the surge of energy to come through you, into you, entering at your root chakra and ascending up your spinal column to your crown chakra, your soul star chakra, and beyond, connecting you to every soul and spirit that ever existed. As you connect to the flow of energy, try not to judge or evaluate what you feel. Just let it all be, now. Resist the need to understand what you feel. The invitation opening to you now is one of a much higher consciousness, where your mere presence is your offering. The days of having to "do" something or "earn" something are behind you. Here, you are the child letting your mothers nourish you and reconnect you to a source of life force energy you may have never experienced.

It is time to unschool yourself, for the ways you have learned for gathering energy through social norms, structures, and conventions have emerged from a patriarchal system where some win and, by definition, others must lose. In this new world of energetic space and connection, all win and no one loses. You do not have more energy than anyone else, nor do you need more. You have everything you need, and so does everyone else. In this place, you are welcome to drink until you are hydrated, eat until you are full, receive until you are satisfied. Here, you will learn only to take what is needed, for you are no longer trying to fill an empty well. Here, the only fuel you need is energy, and it comes in many forms, constantly seeking you. There is no need to feel alone, tired, anxious, or insecure. Here, every one of your immediate needs is met. You no longer look around or behind you. At last—at last—you have come home, and you recognize your inherent worth. Enjoy this moment, for it has been a long time coming.

What will your body do, and how will it heal, from this place of perfect peace and fulfillment? When you no longer look outside yourself, or at any other person, with longing or need, what dreams can finally come true? Stay present to your quartz crystal, allowing it to summon and channel the energies without your permission or request. Everything around you is just unfolding with ease. Learn what this looks like. Memorize what ease feels like. You will need to remember once you unplug from Gaia's immense embrace. She never leaves you, and you never leave her. What you feel now is always available to you. It always has been available to you, waiting for you.

When your energetic gas tank is full and you feel fueled for your journey of love and discovery, release your quartz point from Gaia's skin, from her womb. Call that energy up into your central column and allow it to infuse your energy centers with power, light, and strength. You're disconnecting and unplugging for now, knowing at any time you are welcome to come back and root back in. And this, perhaps, is Gaia's greatest tale of all: Her oldest legend, her first story, is the story of a mother giving birth to her children. We all come from one source, and to her, we shall all, one day, return. You do not own your crystals but are their steward—as they are yours. May you and your crystals serve each other well, in this life and beyond.

And may you both die only one death. May someone continue to speak your names for eternity. Amen, A'ho, and so it is.

NOTES

INTRODUCTION

1 Philemon, H., trans. (1601). C. Plinius Secundus. *The Historie of the World*, Book II.

CHAPTER 2

2 Daniel, Mark. *Inheritance: Covenants, Kingdoms, Bodies, and Nations*. Lulu.com, 2012.

3 Shigley, James. "Historical Reading: The Ancient Emerald Mines of Egypt." Gemological Institute of America. Accessed 2018. www.gia.edu/gia-news-research/historical-reading-ancient-emerald-mines-egypt.

4 Kikas, Jaak. "The Most Mysterious Material—Libyan Desert Glass." 2009. www.looduskalender.ee/en/node/3495.

CHAPTER 3

5 Fobes, Harriet Keith. *Mystic Gems*. R. G. Badger, 1924.

6 Kunz, George Frederick. *The Curious Lore of Precious Stones*. Lippincott, 1913.

CHAPTER 4

7 Shakespeare, William. *Othello*, v.ii. 357–360.

8 Tahil, Patricia, trans. Radcliffe, Joel, ed. *De Virtutibus Lapidum: The Virtures of Stones attributed to Damigeron*. Seattle, WA: Ars Obscura, 1989.

CHAPTER 5

9 Exodus 28:30.

10 Kunz, George Frederick. *The Curious Lore of Precious Stones*. Lippincott, 1913.

11 Kox, Norbert H. *A Speck of Atlantis—Bimini: The Top of God's Mountain*. New Franken, WI: Apocalypse House, 2010.

12 Weiner, Shohama Harris. "Terumah—The Stones of Shoham." Reclaiming Judaism. Accessed 2018. http://reclaimingjudaism.org/teachings/terumah-stones-shoham.

CHAPTER 6

13 Simmons, Robert. "Azeztulite Awakening." Heaven and Earth LLC. Accessed 2018. http://heavenandearthjewelry.com/Azeztulite-Awakening-Robert-Simmons.aspx.

14 Simmons, Robert, and Ahsian, Naisha. *The Book of Stones: Who They Are and What They Teach*. Berkeley, CA: North Atlantic Books, 2007.

CHAPTER 8

15 Kunz, George Frederick. *The Curious Lore of Precious Stones*. Lippincott, 1913.

ABOUT THE AUTHOR

ATHENA PERRAKIS is the founder and CEO of Sage Goddess, the world's largest source of sacred tools and metaphysical education. She holds a Ph.D. in educational leadership and was a professor and executive coach before she founded Sage Goddess. She blends her training in Shamanism, aromatherapy, Reiki, world history, linguistics, comparative religion, and leadership to bring a perspective that is both theoretical and practical.

Athena feels strongly that all spiritual paths are, in fact, One Path moving in the same direction, working toward the same goals, and anchored in the same history. Her desire to find a common thread and unite the world around their common experiences has inspired many people to connect with their own roots and find healing, forgiveness, and peace. By seeking the presence of Source within and honoring one's own divinity, one effortlessly finds beauty in the world.

The Sage Goddess community on Facebook includes 700,000 fans from around the world who are seeking the path to integrated spirituality. Sage Goddess is headquartered in Los Angeles, California, and has a storefront where visitors can meditate, shop for sacred tools, and experience live ritual each month at the full moon.

ACKNOWLEDGMENTS

This book is a labor of love and gratitude—an homage to the Earth's great Crystalline Kingdom, of which I am both guardian and beneficiary. Thanks first to them. This book would not exist if they did not also exist, demanding an accurate account of their lives, their formations, their magic, and their potential to heal. To Jill Alexander, my editor, and to Meredith Quinn, who edited this book with such love and sacred intention. Both of you believed in this project and guided it, and me, toward its becoming. I am indebted to you both. To team SG, and Claire and Alexys in particular, thank you for creating space and helping to make sure the images captured the essence of the writing. I love you both.

I have been guided as a Stone Keeper by many souls but none more profound than the plant and spirit teachers who, in their invisible silence, have taught me all there is to know and more. I am here, you are here, we are here, and on we go. Nick and Zoe, it is your lineage woven into these words. And David, I am thankful for your very being. Know that I love you beyond what words can describe. To our Sage Goddess team and communities, this is *your* history. The stone people are your allies in this life. Don't hesitate to call on them. They have fought many battles and survived.

They stand in your service now.

A'ho and on we go,

Athena

INDEX